EARLY CHILDHOOD EDUCATION SERIES

Leslie R. Williams, Editor

ADVISORY BOARD: Barbara T. Bowman, Harriet K. Cuffaro, Stephanie Feeney, Doris Pronin Fromberg, Celia Genishi, Stacie G. Goffin, Dominic F. Gullo, Alice Sterling Honig, Elizabeth Jones, Gwen Morgan, David Weikart

(Continued)

The Emotional Development of Young Children

BUILDING AN EMOTION-CENTERED CURRICULUM

Second Edition

Marilou Hyson

Foreword by Edward Zigler

Teachers College, Columbia University
New York and London

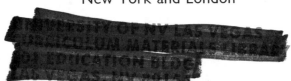

Published by Teachers College Press, 1234 Amsterdam Avenue, New York, NY 10027

Copyright © 2004 by Teachers College, Columbia University

Foreword copyright © 2004 by Edward Zigler

Cover photograph by Maximillian Gretsch. Photographs opening Chapters 1, 2, 4, 5, 6, 7, and Exploration 3 by Jean-Claude Lejeune. Other chapter opening photographs are as follows: Chapter 3 by Francis Wardle, Exploration 1 by Bill Geiger, and Exploration 2 by Marilyn Nolt.

Library of Congress Cataloging-in-Publication Data

Hyson, Marilou.
  The emotional development of young children : building an emotion-centered curriculum / Marilou Hyson.—2nd ed.
    p. cm.—(Early childhood education series)
  Includes bibliographical references and index.
  ISBN 0-8077-4342-9 (pbk.)
    1. Early childhood education—Curricula—United States.   2. Child psychology—United States.   3. Emotions in children.   4. Curriculum planning—United States.   I. Title.   II. Early childhood education series (Teachers College Press)

LB1139.4.H97 2003
372.19—dc21   2003054001

ISBN 0-8077-4342-9 (paper)

Printed on acid-free paper

Manufactured in the United States of America

11 10 09 08 07 06 05 04   8 7 6 5 4 3 2 1

Contents

Foreword

The second edition of this important book could not appear at a more opportune time. When the first edition was published, there was growing acceptance among policy makers that early childhood professionals were right in designing programs to foster children's social and emotional development as well as their cognitive skills. They were convinced by reports that the early years lay the socioemotional foundation for later learning and school success (Zero to Three, 1992), and that Head Start's "whole child" approach to early childhood development was a proven model worthy of emulation (e.g., Schorr, 1988). When Congress reauthorized the nation's largest early intervention program (Head Start Act of 1998), they officially adopted school readiness as the program's goal, defining readiness in terms of physical and mental health, preacademic skills, social and emotional development, and parent involvement.

Since then, there has been a sea change in policy regarding young children's learning. The new buzzwords are literacy, numeracy, and cognitive development. The first White House Conference on children's issues of the twenty-first century was focused on cognitive development—not human development nor, as it turned out, on the whole of cognitive development either. The emphasis was on literacy, one cognitive skill out of many that have been identified as important for success in school. Today many appear to believe that literacy is the only skill a child needs in life and that social and emotional abilities are useless in the serious task of preparing for school.

Cognitive development is, of course, important. But literacy is only one part of cognition, and cognition is only one part of a human being. A child who begins kindergarten knowing letters, sounds, and numbers may be cognitively prepared, but if he or she does not understand how to listen, share, take turns, and get along with teachers and classmates, further learning is jeopardized. Children learn all of these skills through play, which also provides opportunities for acquiring many cognitive skills as well.

Adults are often warned about the dangers of all work and no play, and most realize that all play and no work isn't fruitful either. For young children, however, play *is* their work. Through play they acquire vocabulary, concepts, self-confidence, motivation, and an awareness of the personalities and needs of others. These items are just as important in learning to read as recognizing letters or sounds.

Marilou Hyson has done a splendid job of bringing together the present state of our knowledge of child development and the best of early childhood practice, and combining these with her own creative ideas to help today's educators design an "emotion-centered" curriculum. Her approach makes it clear that such a curriculum is not at odds with ones written to address cognitive development. Rather, the educational processes described integrate the child's social, emotional, and intellectual learning that together foster school readiness.

The research base for the book's recommendations has been updated to reflect the many new studies and research syntheses since the publication of the first edition in 1994. The amount of work that has been done in this area in the decade between editions alone speaks to the importance that developmental scientists and early education professionals attach to children's socioemotional development. Another timely addition is discussion of the growing movement toward early learning standards in the states with attention to how states are (and are not) addressing emotional development in their prekindergarten programs and standards. This current, comprehensive, and highly readable book should help early childhood practitioners in both public and private sectors to develop programs that nurture the whole child and thus foster genuine school readiness.

Edward Zigler
Sterling Professor of Psychology Emeritus
Yale University

REFERENCES

Schorr, L. B. (1988). *Within our reach: Breaking the cycle of disadvantage.* New York: Doubleday.
Zero to Three: National Center for Clinical Infant Programs. (1992). *Heart start: The emotional foundations of school readiness.* Arlington, VA: Author.

Acknowledgments

Writing about emotions is an emotional process—no less so with the second edition of this book than with the first. As readers will see, my theoretical perspectives on emotional development continue to be strongly influenced by Carroll Izard's ground-breaking scholarship; less evident but no less important have been his generosity, good will, and collaborative spirit. Elizabeth Foster Stonorov, who founded Charlestown Play House over 60 years ago, exerts a quietly inspiring influence on my beliefs about emotion-centered programs for young children—and provides a caring place for my grandson Samuel Nelson Hyson to begin his early education journey.

My visits to the excellent early childhood settings described in the first edition of this book remain fresh and even more relevant today. I especially acknowledge and honor the contributions of master practitioners Jane Davidson, Nancy Edwards, Nadine Heim, Charlotte Holden, Colleen Katzman, Faithe Koser, and Judy McGlothlin. Sadly, I join their many colleagues and friends in mourning the untimely deaths of Jane Davidson and Judy McGlothlin, who influenced countless young children, families, and practitioners.

This second edition would not have been possible without the support and patience of Susan Liddicoat of Teachers College Press and of NAEYC's staff, including Executive Director Mark Ginsberg and Publications Editor Carol Copple. My heightened awareness of public policy and advocacy, reflected in this edition, have been nurtured and stimulated by NAEYC's Adele Robinson and by Naomi Karp's guidance during my fellowship year in the U.S. Department of Education's National Institute on Early Childhood Development and Education. NAEYC staff Kristine von Brook, Heather Benson, and intern Karen Curtis gave me invaluable, just-in-time practical assistance with manuscript preparation. I owe special thanks to NAEYC's intern Christopher Maring, whose competence was instrumental in updating references and resources. I hope that my colleagues in state departments of education, other professional associations, and higher education will know the extent of my gratitude for their generosity in sharing their current concerns, issues, and initiatives. Readers of this edition are the beneficiaries.

Since the publication of this book's first edition, my own emotional connections have multiplied. Not only John, Jeff, and Dan, but now Juliette, Jess, and dear Sammy and Ellie never let me forget where emotional development finds its true center.

The Emotional Development of Young Children

BUILDING AN EMOTION-CENTERED CURRICULUM

Introduction: Young Children's Emotions and Early Childhood Education

It's Monday of the second week of preschool. As the 2-year-olds arrive with their parents, Natalie greets each of them at the door.

"Hi, how are you, Adam?" (accompanied by a quick stroke of Adam's hair) Then Adam is off to investigate his new love, the bathroom sink. "Hey, Zach, how *are* you?" "You're going to stay and play with us today, Felicia." "Sarah! How are *you*? Oh, look at that!" Most of the children come in holding large sheets of paper, to which are pasted photographs with printed captions. The week before, each child had made an individual "me and my family" poster using pictures that parents had sent in. The posters had been sent home over the weekend for the children to share with their families. As the children hand their posters to Natalie, she carefully places each one in a growing stack on the radiator. One child is clutching his poster especially tightly. Natalie says, "We'll put your name on this, Ben, so we'll know it's yours."

As the children enter, many of them spontaneously find things to do. Simple activities have been set out: easel painting, play dough, doll beds with dolls and accessories, Legos, and little cars. Natalie walks over to the play dough table. "Michael found the play dough. Where are your fingers, Michael?" she says playfully. "Are your fingers hiding underneath there?"

Natalie moves back toward the doorway. Jessica is standing halfway into the room, leaning against her mother. Tyrone approaches Natalie with a dishpan full of Legos. Natalie says to Tyrone, "I think Jessica really likes to do that. Maybe she would do it with you."

In a nearby kindergarten, the children have just finished a free-choice time like the one in Natalie's class. Now Christine's kindergarten children are sitting in a circle. A book lies on the rug in front of each child. The children have been talking about the books they selected. They have been describing the pictures on the covers and speculating about what stories might be inside them. Lowering her voice intriguingly, Christine says to the children, "You see lots of different things about your books. Here's another question: What's the *same* about books?" After a few false starts, Brian offers, "They all have pages!"

As the discussion proceeds, Aaron is the only child who does not pay any attention. Seated beside Christine, Aaron has been gazing at his fingers, wiggling his hands, and twisting around looking at the ceiling and at the bulletin board behind him. Christine has occasionally touched his arm or gently rubbed his back. Now Aaron flops over and waves his legs in the air. Christine leans toward him and says in a quiet, friendly tone, "Aaron, please sit up and give Brian your attention and respect."

The discussion of book characteristics continues. Maria looks around at the books on the rug, thinks for a minute, and says, "All books have covers." Christine's face takes on an expression of surprise and pleasure. She looks impressed. "Did you all hear what Maria said? She said books have covers!"

The group meeting ends, and the children prepare to go outside. As Christine goes around the circle, collecting a book from each child, she looks each child in the eyes and manages to create a brief personal contact.

Several children are still paging through their books. "Jameela, would you like me to put that book on the bookshelf for you next week?" Christine asks one reader. Jameela nods enthusiastically. Laughing with delight, Christine comments to the class as a whole, "We *like* books! I think books are our *friends*!"

A BOOK ABOUT EMOTIONS

Although set in the world of early childhood education, this book is not about early literacy. It is not about mathematical reasoning. It is not even about social competence or about effective instructional practices. And yet it is about all these things because it is about emotions—the joy, sadness, fear, interest, anger, shame, and surprise that color and motivate children's early development, learning, and relationships.

Many early childhood professionals have always believed that children's emotions are central to their lives and should be central to the curriculum. However, in recent years these beliefs have been eroded. Early childhood programs often feel pressured to adopt a curriculum focused exclusively on mastery of cognitive skills. This narrow curriculum is frequently accompanied by formal, emotionally detached relationships between teachers and young children—relationships made more distant by teachers' fears of accusations of sexual abuse. In this climate early childhood professionals who continue to advocate for an emotion-centered curriculum can sound apologetic, defensive, or out of step with scientific research.

Ironically, during this same period developmental psychologists have taken a different path, one that is more consistent with the deep-seated beliefs and preferences of many early childhood professionals. The last 20 years have witnessed a remarkable revival of interest in the study of emotions and of early emotional development, subjects that had been virtually ignored in previous decades. Using innovative research methods and building on earlier theoretical models, a new generation of researchers has documented emotions' importance as organizers of children's behavior and learning, and as essential components of school readiness and academic success (e.g., Denham, 1998; Izard, 1991; Lemerise & Arsenio, 2000; Saarni, Mumme, & Campos, 1998; Thompson, 1994). This knowledge base can provide a solid foundation for rebuilding an emotion-centered early childhood curriculum.

COMPONENTS OF THE EMOTION-FOCUSED TRADITION IN EARLY CHILDHOOD EDUCATION

Early childhood education has a long history. A major part of that history has been a long-standing concern with young children's emotional development. Appendix A summarizes the historical roots of that tradition and suggests further reading on the topic.

Traditionally (though not always consciously), early childhood programs have emphasized five emotion-related components: the emotional nature of teacher-child relationships; activities to meet children's emotional needs; open expression of feelings by children and adults; the development of positive affective states and dispositions; and awareness of children's emotional responses. As Christine and Natalie begin the new school year, they incorporate all of these elements into their programs.

Emotional Bonds Between Teacher and Child

Early childhood programs have traditionally valued the emotional relationship between children and their teachers. Like many of her fellow early childhood professionals, Natalie's first priority is to build a trusting, emotionally positive bond between herself and the children. Natalie makes certain that each child's basic needs are met promptly and lovingly. Children are touched, held, and helped to feel valued and needed. Natalie skillfully bridges family and school by encouraging parents to stay for a while during the first week and by giving family members and children tasks to complete together, pictures that can then be brought to school and proudly shared. The class "book" that will be made from these posters will literally bind together home and school experiences, as well as individual and group feelings, in a concrete and emotionally meaningful way.

Christine, too, is forging personal emotional links with her kindergartners as they begin the new year. Creating an intimate atmosphere, Christine gets physically close to the children, even during an "academic" activity such as this minilesson about books, titles, and authors. Her manner is warm and friendly as she begins to construct individual relationships with the children, sharing small jokes and gently teasing those who enjoy it. When she has to remind a child of the classroom rules, she does so in a personal way. Her words and behavior suggest that she will be a resource, an enthusiastic cheerleader, and a supportive guide for the children as they embark on learning in the kindergarten.

Activities to Meet Children's Emotional Needs

Natalie offers the 2-year-olds materials and activities that assist in all areas of development. However, emotional development is always a high priority, and it takes on special significance at this point in the year. Natalie's activities seem designed to heighten children's positive attitudes about coming to school, to help children master separation-related feelings, to provide sensory enjoyment, and to offer opportunities for pleasurable social interaction. For example, Natalie had rigged a long cardboard tube so that it hung from ceiling hooks and could be tilted at various angles. During the first week of school, many children were drawn to the tube, tipping it, peering into it, and placing small cars in the openings, gleefully watching them emerge at the other end. In addition to its obvious value for cognitive and language development, the tube activity afforded rich opportunities for children to reexperience disappearance and reappearance, which is an emotionally charged issue at the beginning of the year.

Like Natalie's cardboard tube activity, Christine's book sharing is emotionally, as well as intellectually, satisfying. The children selected their books individually and were invited to share things about their books with other children. The children's careful handling of the books and their eagerness to tell about their own selections showed that they were beginning to develop a personal connection with books and the reading process—an essential foundation for reading success. Christine structured the activity to meet the kindergartners' need for recognition and acceptance by the group. She explicitly directed children's attention to "good ideas" and interesting comments offered by their classmates, encouraging children to admire one another's abilities.

Encouraging Open Expression of Feelings

Another persistent theme in early education has been the encouragement of emotion expression. Children's feelings, even "negative" emotions, are accepted and respected.

Several 2-year-olds cried during the first week of school. Tears and sobs came when their parents left and at transition times during the day. Natalie acknowledged children's sadness and offered hugs, soothing words, and tissues as needed. Natalie also encouraged and reflected children's expressions of happiness, curiosity, and surprise, as they explored the play dough, the cardboard tube, and other activities in the room.

With the kindergarten children, Christine's priority seems to be to encourage children to express positive feelings about learning. Christine creates an emotionally expressive environment in which learning activities become sources of curiosity, excitement, and sometimes frustration. Open in her own expression of feelings, Christine models a lively affective style that begins to permeate the classroom.

Developing Desirable Emotional States and Dispositions

Early childhood education has traditionally emphasized "emotion socialization"—helping children to learn desirable ways of expressing feelings and helping them to develop healthy patterns of understanding and regulating emotions.

Natalie's selection of activities and materials, and her involvement with the children during this brief observation, hint at some of her priorities. She encourages the development of trust, independence, warm friendships, and a sense of unity and fellowship among the children. At one point, a child, upon hearing the name of another child in the class (Jessica), said she had a sister named Jessica. Hearing this, Natalie commented, "Now you have a *friend* Jessica *and* a sister Jessica."

Like Natalie, Christine encourages positive feelings about school. More specifically, she works on developing feelings of interest and joy about the increasingly challenging cognitive tasks the children will encounter over the next few years. Christine's comment that "books are our *friends*" made this theme explicit. On a commercial poster, this phrase might be a cliché. However, Christine's spontaneous exclamation served to throw open the door to a year of literacy experiences filled with joy, effort, surprise, and emotional satisfaction.

With her kindergarten children, Christine expects more self-regulation of emotion expression than Natalie expects from the 2-year-olds. Christine's interaction with Aaron typifies the way she begins to establish class norms about listening to other children, showing respect for classmates, and being kind to others.

Awareness of Children's Emotional Responses

Emotional development has held a strong fascination for many early childhood practitioners and researchers. Children's emotional reactions are frequently the subject of teachers' conversations, observations, and informal study.

Natalie supervises several student teachers, with whom she talks over classroom events after the children leave each day. Topics in these postsessions are broad ranging, but they often emphasize emotion-related issues such as children's reactions to separation, their interest in activities, or their formation of emotional attachments to adults and children in the class.

Christine takes obvious pleasure in watching how her kindergartners react to the new activities and tasks of the first few weeks of school. Her eyes continually dart around the room as she seeks information about children's responses. When one talks with Christine about the children in her class, it is evident that she thinks of them in highly individual terms. She knows her children's abilities in the cognitive domain, but she also integrates that knowledge with perceptive observation of each child's unique affective engagement with social and academic tasks.

EMOTIONS TODAY

Christine and Natalie reflect a long tradition of emphasis on emotions in early childhood programs. But is this typical of current practice? What is the status of emotions in today's early childhood programs? Although teachers like Christine and Natalie reflect a strong commitment to emotional development as a priority, most professionals agree that neglect of emotions and negative influences on emotional development have recently dominated much of early childhood education.

Neglect and Negativity

In a social policy report from the Society for Research in Child Development, Raver (2002) concludes that "psychologists' and educators' emphasis on cognition and on children's academic preparedness continues to overshadow the importance of children's social and emotional development for early school readiness" (p. 3). Other national reports echo this concern (Peth-Pierce, 2000; Raver & Knitzer, 2002; Shonkoff & Phillips, 2001). This tendency to ignore or deny emotions even extends to programs for those most in need of close relationships—infants and toddlers, including those with disabilities (Frede, Barnett, & Lupo, 2001; Leavitt, 1994). Harshness is not the only danger. In *The Erosion of Childhood*, Polakow (1992) described 2 years of participant observations in five nursery school and child care programs. Her book offers a detailed ethnographic portrait of teachers who created bland, affectively sanitized environments and who manipulated children's emotions to serve adult ends. Teachers often responded to children in what Polakow judged to be emotionally false ways, appearing to "deny the angry intentions of the children" and masking "the outward manifestations of their own anger or irritation" (pp. 86–87). Polakow argued that these emotionally sterile programs are typical of broader trends in American child care. She may be right. National studies of child care quality (Cost, Quality, & Child Outcomes Study Team, 1995) have found widespread emotional insensitivity, detachment, and even harshness among early childhood teachers.

Reasons for Neglect

What accounts for these trends? Certainly the low wages and poor working conditions in the early childhood field have created conditions in which many early childhood teachers have minimal education and training about young children's needs, and in which more than a third of all early childhood teachers leave their positions each year. Two other factors have also been influential. Since the 1980s, early childhood programs have experienced ever-greater expectations from families and policy makers to focus on academic skills at younger and younger ages. Second, a series of widely reported cases of sexual abuse in child care, most publicized in the 1980s, have had a continuing ripple effect that has made many professionals and parents cautious about teachers' expressions of affection. Together, these concerns have helped to push emotions to the back burner of early education.

An overwhelming focus on academic standards, outcomes, and accountability pressures in early childhood programs has surely contributed to an educational climate that ignores emotional competence. There is no *necessary* relationship between an emphasis on academic competence and an unemotional or emotionally negative classroom climate—intellectual challenge and emotional support seem natural partners (Hyson, 2003). However, in real life a different picture appears: Hyson, Hirsh-Pasek, and Rescorla (1990) found that preschool programs that emphasized teacher-directed formal academic instruction (using few concrete materials and offering children few choices of activities) were much less likely to be rated as having a positive emotional climate. In contrast to teachers whose programs offered more child choice and firsthand experiences, teachers with a more abstract, formally academic, adult-directed program talked little about feelings, were not physically affectionate, and tended to use competition and negative comparison rather than redirection as discipline strategies.

Stipek and colleagues have found similar results in their research (Stipek & Greene, 2001). In observations of the programs and emotional tone in numerous child care settings, a highly didactic, teacher-dominated curriculum was almost invariably accompanied by lower amounts of teacher warmth and responsiveness and by more negative approaches to dealing with misbehavior.

Even in the absence of high academic pressures, teachers' concerns about sexual abuse may influence their emotion-related attitudes and behaviors. Many early childhood professionals acknowledge that they sometimes hold back from being physically affectionate with children because of fear that this behavior will be misinterpreted. Their fears may have some basis: Hyson, Whitehead, and Prudhoe (1988) showed parents and other adults a videotape of scenes in which adults interacted with young children in a normal, friendly way. Some viewers were told that the adults on the tape were child care providers, and some scenes included normal affectionate touches between the adults and the children. Viewers were asked to indicate how much they approved of each scene. Viewers were more disapproving of adult-child physical affection if they thought the adults were child care providers rather than parents, and if the physically affectionate adult was male.

The Effects of Neglecting Emotions

Early childhood environments that ignore emotions or create emotionally detached or harsh relationships with children have negative effects both on children's later socioemotional development and on their cognitive competence. Insecure or conflicted relationships with child care and kindergarten teachers are linked to later social and academic problems (Hamre & Pianta, 2001; Howes & Ritchie, 2002). Children who enter school with emotional difficulties, unable to regulate their anger or distress, are unready to learn—emotional competence is at least as much a part of school readiness as literacy or mathematical skills. Children who cannot understand or name their own feelings or those of others have less capacity to develop empathy; in addition, they have less positive behavioral and academic outcomes (Schultz, Izard, Ackerman, & Youngstrom, 2001). A series of studies have shown that in the long run children with continuing emotional difficulties, especially with anger and aggression, become more likely to drop out of school and engage in antisocial or delinquent activities (Raver, 2002). Thus the neglect of emotions can place young children on a negative trajectory, affecting their chances for success in both the socioemotional and academic arenas.

Beyond Neglect—Tools from the Field

The need for a renewed attention to emotions and emotional competence has never been greater. If children are to be, as the first National Education Goal says, "ready to learn" (National Education Goals Panel, 1997), they must have the underlying security and emotional foundations for that learning, and for the later social and emotional tasks necessary for success and satisfaction in life. Yet "few school reform movements have paid much attention to the social and emotional components in reforming schools" (Bowman, 1999, p. 285), even when family, community, and political violence and trauma place even more children at risk for emotional difficulties.

Fortunately, 20 years of research provide convincing evidence of the importance of emotions in early development and learning—and about the role that adults and affective environments play in supporting emotional competence. As described in later chapters of this book, these researchers make several important points:

1. Emotions are the principal guides and motivators of behavior and learning from infancy throughout life.
2. Both positive and negative emotions—joy, interest, surprise, as well as sadness, anger, and fear—play important roles in development.
3. Young children's ability to express, understand, and regulate their emotions follows typical developmental sequences or pathways.
4. Both biological and environmental factors influence that pathway—temperament, culture, relationships with adults and peers, and many other factors come into play throughout childhood and beyond.

An underlying message of all this research is that emotional development is too important to be left to chance. Adults, including early childhood professionals, can make the difference, supporting positive development, being alert to possible problems, and intervening early and effectively.

ABOUT THIS BOOK

In preparing a second edition of this book, I have sought to strengthen the emotional component of the reform agenda in early childhood education. The book follows the National Association for the Education of Young Children (NAEYC) in defining *early childhood* as spanning the years from birth to age 8. Therefore, the early childhood program settings referred to in this book include child care centers and family child care homes, early intervention programs of many kinds, part-day and full-day preschools, kindergartens, and primary-grade classes. For this reason, the word *teachers* includes a broad array of professional roles—classroom teachers, family child care providers, home visitors, family support personnel, and other specialists. Similarly, the young children in the book represent the rich spectrum of age, culture, ethnicity, family environment, and individual temperament that early childhood professionals encounter and welcome in their work. Finally, young children with disabilities are integrated into the book as they are—or should be—in early childhood programs.

The book does not provide detailed guidance in working with children who have serious emotional difficulties. The classroom examples and research summarized in later chapters emphasize typical developmental and individual patterns. However, many of the book's recommended strategies can be adapted to the special needs of children with social and emotional disabilities.

Part I uses scenes from the classrooms and family child care homes of skilled practitioners to introduce the essential components of a curriculum that promotes emotional development. Chapter 1 begins with an overview of the emotion-centered curriculum. The next six chapters draw on current research and many examples of sound professional practices to focus in detail on each of six goals that support emotional competence in early childhood.

In each chapter, Resource Notes—a new feature in the second edition—extend and complement the text with examples of recent developments in early childhood policies and programs, self-assessment questions for practitioners, and other practical tools.

Although each chapter in Part I relies on and refers to theory and research that support these goals, some readers may wish to go into this background in more depth. The explorations in Part II, another new feature of the second edition, are designed with this purpose in mind. Each of the three explorations begins with a brief vignette and then poses a series of questions about a specific topic for reflection and discussion with colleagues or fellow students. Summaries of key information about the topic, and an annotated set of significant readings, support these explorations.

The four new appendices at the end of the book provide several additional resources. These include information about the emotion-based traditon in early childhood education, suggestions for classroom-based interventions that support young children's emotional skills, a table of links between this book's content and two important sections of the Head Start Child Outcomes Framework, and a guide to selected assessment tools.

MEETING THE PRACTITIONERS

Seven early childhood professionals—Natalie, Christine, Hope, Terry, Denise, Ilene, and Leslie—are featured in the chapters and explorations to follow. Although descriptions of their backgrounds, programs, and teaching styles combine features from several sources, and although details have been changed to protect adults' and children's privacy, these portrayals are based on real people.

We have already met Natalie and Christine, whose classrooms in a university laboratory school we will visit in Part I. *Natalie* teaches 2- and 3-year-olds. Each year children with disabilities are included in her program. Natalie has also worked in early intervention programs and in infant child care, and she continues to involve herself in training for infant and toddler caregivers.

Christine now teaches kindergarten children, after several years of working in an urban alternative elementary school. Her class includes children with identified disabilities. Many of her children have parents who teach or hold staff positions at the university, and a number are from other countries.

Three other early childhood professionals are also featured in the chapters in Part I. *Hope* is a teacher in a public elementary school located in a rural area. She teaches a multiage primary-grade class with a wide range of developmental levels and with a number of children of migrant families whose home language is Spanish. Hope has also taught in kindergarten and in a public school prekindergarten program. Her multiage class has been the focus of much community interest this year.

Terry is a family child care provider in a suburban/rural area. With the help of her sister-in-law and, occasionally, her husband, she cares for 11 children ranging from 6 months to 4 years in age, including 2-year-old triplets. Her children's families are Latino, African American, and European American, and one of the triplets has a chronic medical condition.

Denise teaches 2- and 3-year-olds in an urban child care center that serves predominantly African American families. Many of the children's families have limited incomes and are single-parent families. Her center has an active foster grandparent program and a strong emphasis on family involvement.

The explorations in Part II draw on the work of Ilene and Leslie. *Ilene* teaches 4-year-olds in a Head Start program and is actively involved in staff development. Her many years of experience in this program were preceded by work in a parent cooperative preschool. Ilene is known for her careful observations of children's behavior and for her commitment to fostering pretend play in her classroom.

Leslie is a family child care provider in a suburban community. Many of her children have stayed with her from the first months of their lives through their transition to elementary school. Leslie has a background in nursing and has become a leader in promoting the professional development of family child care providers.

The practitioners featured in this book are diverse in every way but one: They are all women. In this respect they represent the overwhelming majority of early childhood professionals. However, this book's recommendations are not gender specific. Both men and women nurture young children's emotional development, in families and in early childhood programs.

Entering their profession with diverse backgrounds and working in diverse settings, Natalie, Christine, Hope, Terry, Denise, Ilene, and Leslie represent a uniformly high level of commitment to excellent early childhood programs with a strong emphasis on emotional development. However, my descriptions of their approaches to teaching are not intended to serve as a "cookbook." I hope, instead, that readers will construct their own understanding of the emotion-centered curriculum from these materials, their individual experiences, and their personal values.

Now that we have met the entire group of practitioners, Natalie and her 2-year-olds will guide us toward an overview of the defining features of an emotion-centered curriculum.

PART I

CONSTRUCTING AN EMOTION-CENTERED CURRICULUM

This part of *The Emotional Development of Young Children* gives a detailed picture of the essential features of an emotion-centered curriculum, enriched by numerous examples from five practitioners: Natalie, Hope, Terry, Christine, and Denise. These examples, the descriptions of the theoretical and research base for the chapters' recommendations, and the Resource Notes included in each chapter aim to stimulate reflection, discussion, and application.

Chapter 1 provides an overview of the emotion-centered curriculum including the teacher's role, the place of academic content, and adaptations for different age groups, settings, and individual needs. After this overview, the remaining six chapters describe specific teaching goals and strategies: creating a secure emotional environment (Chapter 2); helping children to understand emotions (Chapter 3); modeling genuine, appropriate emotional responses (Chapter 4); supporting children's regulation of emotions (Chapter 5); recognizing and honoring children's expressive styles (Chapter 6); and uniting children's learning with positive emotions (Chapter 7).

Chapter 1

The Emotion-Centered Curriculum: An Overview

The 2-year-olds have been playing together for about an hour. On this day, many children cluster around a table where they can use foam rubber shapes to make collages. The children seem fascinated with peeling off the paper to expose the sticky backing of the foam circles and squares. Natalie, the teacher, sits on a low chair near the table. Several children lean comfortably against her as they examine the collage materials.

A few other children are over at the bulletin board, which today has been covered with a sheet of contact paper, sticky side out. Children are choosing pieces of yarn, colored paper, and cloth from a box on the floor and sticking the materials to the bulletin board. Other children work at spreading apple butter on miniature bagels that will be served at snack time.

These 2-year-olds are not big talkers, but Natalie keeps up a flow of conversation and commentary on the children's doings. "Carl, can you help Erin turn the water on?" "Here's the orange paper you wanted, Mandy. Did you want to finish your picture now or later?" "Do you hear what Aaron is saying to you? He's saying no." "Krystal, are you happy today?" Natalie asks as Krystal walks by with her arms over her head. "Aaron, did you go in the tunnel? Is it dark in there? Aaron's going in again. I won't see him now. Oh, there he is back again!"

Besides participating in the activities that have been set out, some children work intently on self-chosen missions. Paulina spends several minutes struggling to get some play dough out of a plastic bag set into a large container. When she gets her piece she smiles with satisfaction. Next, she works at opening the latch on a lunch box that she found in a cupboard. Once she manages to open the lunch box, she pulls small pieces off her lump of play dough and carefully places them inside. Carrying her lunch box, Paulina crosses the room to a wooden riding bench placed in the block area. She sits contentedly on the riding bench, turning the steering wheel. "There goes Paulina on her trip," says Natalie to several children at the collage table. "Send us a postcard, Paulina. *Adios*! Bye, bye!" Paulina gives a small wave and a pleased smile from her perch across the room. The whole enterprise has taken more than 10 minutes.

Loud growling comes from inside a plastic tunnel. Carl peers out with a fierce expression, growls even more loudly, and retreats into the tunnel. Several children look a little alarmed. After a few minutes, Natalie walks over to the tunnel, sits down, talks quietly to Carl, and returns to the collage table. Softer growls come from the tunnel.

Several puzzles and small shape-sorting toys have been put out on the rug. Krystal and Aaron lie flat on the floor, working on opening a plastic house. Using a color-matched key, Aaron opens one of the doors and pulls out two miniature people. "My daddy!" Aaron exclaims. And "My mommy!" as he finds another figure. He extends them toward Natalie as he scrambles up from the floor and approaches her. "Oh, Aaron, look at the mommy and daddy," says Natalie as Aaron presses them together. "Are they hugging each other?" Aaron nods with conviction.

Even a short visit to Natalie's 2-year-old program shows that the curriculum is truly emotion-centered. Of course, young children's behavior and learning are always motivated by emotions. In this sense, every early childhood program is emotion-centered. In this book, however, the term *emotion-centered curriculum* is reserved for programs that *deliberately*, *positively*, and *reflectively* use emotions as a starting point in designing experiences to support every aspect of young children's development.

An emotion-centered early childhood curriculum explicitly recognizes the central importance of emotions in young children's development. As research shows (see Resource Note 1.1), the development of emotional competence is an essential foundation for effective academic and social functioning (Bowman, Donovan, & Burns, 2001; Lewis, 1998; Peth-Pierce, 2000; Raver, 2002; Salovey & Sluyter, 1997; Shields et al., 2001).

Curriculum planners use current knowledge of emotions to make informed decisions about curriculum goals, selection of activities, teacher-child interactions, and assessment of children's progress. This chapter will describe the basic ingredients of an emotion-centered curriculum, recognizing that each teacher mixes these ingredients with a personal style. In presenting these ingredients, I also will address some real-world concerns expressed by practitioners who are considering a more emotion-focused approach to early childhood education. I will try to show that this approach is consistent with current thinking about early learning standards, curriculum, and teaching practices, enhancing rather than undermining the development of academic skills. Finally, the chapter will recommend some steps practitioners might take to "refocus" on emotions.

INGREDIENTS OF AN EMOTION-CENTERED CURRICULUM

Every early childhood program is different. Differences in children, staff, and settings combine to create unique ecologies. Nevertheless, emotion-centered programs will have certain distinctive ingredients. Visiting a classroom like Natalie's, a perceptive observer will notice certain hallmarks or clues that this is indeed an emotion-centered program.

Emotional Engagement

In an emotion-centered program, children are emotionally engaged in their life at school. This does not mean that every child displays a big smile throughout the day; constant "fun" is not the goal of an emotion-centered curriculum. But most of the time, children's faces, voices, and bodies indicate a high level of absorption and emotional involvement. Whether peeling the backing off a foam rubber disk, spreading apple butter on bagels, crawling through a tunnel, or trying out different ways to unlock the doors of the plastic dollhouse, the children in Natalie's class (like

---

RESOURCE NOTE 1.1 The Emotional Side of School Readiness

Major national reports, federal agencies, and private foundations have recognized that children's emotional competence is an essential ingredient of school readiness.

- *A Good Beginning: Sending America's Children to School with the Social and Emotional Competence They Need to Succeed* (Peth-Pierce, 2000) summarizes research showing that later socioemotional *and* academic success can be predicted from early emotional and social competence. Based on papers commissioned by a network of mental health agencies and foundations, the report recommends greater attention to this aspect of early education and teacher preparation (*http://www.nimh.nih.gov/childhp/monograph.pdf*).
- The Child Care Bureau and the Head Start Bureau have supported the creation of a National Center on the Social and Emotional Foundations of Early Learning. With the help of primary partners including the Council for Exceptional Children's Division for Early Childhood (DEC), the National Association for the Education of Young Children (NAEYC), the National Association of Child Care Resource and Referral Agencies (NACCRRA), the National Association of Bilingual Educators (NABE), and the National Black Child Development Institute (NBCDI) the resource center disseminates research findings and effective practices to help practitioners support positive development and prevent later social and emotional difficulties (*http://csefel.uiuc.edu*).
- The Ewing Marion Kauffmann Foundation has given high priority to promoting early emotional development. The inaugural conference of the Kauffman Early Education Exchange series (November 2001) focused on the social and emotional development of young children as an essential building block for school success. A full report and executive summary of the report, *Set for Success: Building a Strong Foundation for School Readiness Based on the Social-Emotional Development of Young Children* (2002), is also available on the foundation's Web site at (*http://www.emkf.org*).
- Two reports echo the same theme for policy makers—an SRCD *Social Policy Report*, "Emotions Matter: Making the Case for the Role of Young Children's Emotional Development for Early School Readiness" (Raver, 2002) (*http://www.srcd.org/spr.html*), and the National Center for Children in Poverty's *Ready to Enter: What Research Tells Policymakers About Strategies to Promote Social and Emotional School Readiness Among Three- and Four-Year-Old Children* (Raver & Knitzer, 2002; *http://cpmcnet.columbia.edu/dept/nccp/ProEmoPP3.html*). Both reports state that well-designed interventions in family and early education settings are sound policy investments, reducing children's later emotional and behavioral problems and promoting readiness for school.

---

other children in emotion-centered programs) display curiosity and interest. As they go about the activities of the day, their faces reflect concentration and involvement: Their brows often furrow in concentration and their lips press together as they focus intensely on the work they have chosen to tackle. Their jaws may drop open and eyes widen in surprise when they experience a new sound or scent, solve a new problem, or produce an unexpected result. From time to time, sounds of glee may punctuate the hum of busy activity. Whether the child is an infant fitting a block into a container or a first grader printing a note to her teacher, an observer will notice focused attention, concentration, and personal satisfaction at the successful completion of tasks.

In programs that use an emotion-centered curriculum, children approach new materials and activities with relish. Children appear optimistic about their ability to figure things out and get help from adults and other children when they need it.

Warm Adult-Child Relationships

In these kinds of classrooms, children's relationships with their teachers are strikingly warm and mutually engaged. Like Mandy, Paulina, Carl, and others in Natalie's class, children approach adults with confidence. They smile at, touch, show things to, and seek assistance, collaboration, and comfort from adults. In turn, teachers appear genuinely delighted by the children, showing spontaneous interest in their activities and sharing their problems and triumphs. The flavor of this relationship certainly varies with the children's ages and with the program's cultural context. Natalie is gentler and more physically comforting with her 2-year-olds than is the kindergarten teacher next door. But whatever the specific situation, adult-child relationships are always characterized by genuine mutual liking and emotional connectedness.

Emotion-centered teachers create relationships that support children's emotional development. They accept children's feelings and respond to their needs for recognition, comfort, and inclusion. "Mandy has a little skiing person on her shirt," Natalie says affectionately, stroking Mandy's sweatshirt and gently turning Mandy so the other children at the table can see. "What happened to your fingers, Helen?" says Natalie, touching Helen's three bandaged fingertips, and adds, "Hi, Kimberly," to a small girl standing diffidently outside a group of children near the table. Natalie's welcoming tone and warm smile included Kimberly in the group without pressuring her to assume center stage.

Direct Expression of Feelings

A visitor to an emotion-centered program sees children express their feelings openly. "I *want* to make this for my mommy," Carl demanded, as he barged into the collage group clutching paper and scissors. Krystal joyously flung her arms over her head in spontaneous pleasure as she walked toward her teacher. Mandy bounced across the room on tiptoes to put her carefully torn pieces of orange paper in her cubby. Individual temperament and cultural standards may influence how intensely children display their emotions, but an emotion-centered curriculum always has room for feelings.

Individual and Cultural Styles

Programs that lack a strong emotional focus may restrict opportunities to develop individual and culturally compatible interests and styles, because children perform activities in only one stereotyped way. In contrast, after only a short time in Natalie's class, a visitor has a clear sense of Ellie's tentativeness, Carl's zestfully expressive manner, and Mandy's warm responsiveness. In an emotion-centered program, teachers value and encourage individuality as well as children's culturally distinctive "collective identities" (Greenfield, 1994). Natalie frequently refers to children's personal desires and interests, showing those children and others in the group that these individual qualities are to be respected and enjoyed. "Ellie, did you want to feed the fish?" "I think Erin wanted to make a reindeer with the play dough cutter. Is that right, Erin?" "Aaron, do you want Sarah to put on two pairs of sunglasses? What do you think, Sarah? Would that be fun to do?" Natalie and other emotion-focused teachers allow children to place their own stamp on activities while remaining sensitive to differences in how individuality is expressed within and between cultures.

Attunement to Others

Despite this encouragement of individuality, children in an emotion-centered program may seem especially tuned in to others' interests, feelings, and needs. This is no accident—teachers actively promote this emotional awareness. Natalie's toddlers are at an age that many teachers regard as hopelessly egocentric. Nevertheless, Natalie supports their growing awareness of others' feelings: "Thanks, Mandy, for passing that to Aaron. He really needed it." "Krystal, she might not want to put that in your lunch box," as Krystal attempts to get Becky to relinquish a piece of paper. "Oh, she *does* want to!" says Natalie warmly and delightedly, as both girls beam with satisfaction over the transaction.

Emotionally Relevant Activities

Intellectual content is essential, but teachers using an emotion-centered curriculum select activities that have emotional relevance for children. Planned and impromptu activities encourage children to talk about, write about, and play about emotionally important issues. Teachers like Natalie know that emotionally relevant activities will build strong links between affective and cognitive development and will result in more persistent, engaged, and enthusiastic learning.

What is emotionally relevant will vary with children's age, culture, and individual needs. Many of Natalie's 2-year-olds are intensely interested in issues of separation and reunion, disappearance and reappearance. In Natalie's classroom, children love the plastic tunnel. Besides its benefits for physical development, it allows children to control their appearances and disappearances and to playfully experience positive and negative feelings. The small dollhouse with its doors, keys, and small people inside engages the 2-year-olds' curiosity and interest not just because of the fine motor skills involved, but because of the children's fascination with retrieving the little human figures hidden inside the house—and then making them disappear again.

Many of the activities in Natalie's room gain their emotional power because they let children have an immediate, personal effect on their environment. Pressing objects into play dough to leave marks, sticking yarn onto the contact paper wall, hammering golf tees into a large block of styrofoam—these and many other activities allow the children to experience the pleasure of being a cause.

It would certainly be possible to find other activities that emphasized the same concepts and skills. However, by selecting emotionally relevant activities, the emotion-centered teacher ensures that children will engage in sustained, purposeful exploration, resulting in cognitive, academic, and emotional benefits.

"YES, BUT . . ."—SOME REAL-WORLD CONCERNS

After reading this description of the core characteristics of an emotion-centered curriculum, some early childhood teachers may still have concerns about its possible shortcomings.

Neglect of Academic Content

"Doesn't this emotional emphasis neglect academic standards and cognitive development? My children have so much catching up to do to get them ready for later success in school. My top priority has to be their academic skills and concepts."

Centering the curriculum on emotions does not require that the entire curriculum must be *about* emotions. Just as "child-centered" does not mean "child-dominated" (Bredekamp & Copple, 1997; Bredekamp & Rosegrant, 1992), "emotion-centered" does not mean "emotion-only." Many researchers find that emotions are the primary motivators and organizers of all development and learning. These writers also emphasize that emotion and cognition are closely linked throughout development, but especially in the early childhood years (Blair, 2002; Lemerise & Arsenio, 2000; Lewis, 1999). Thus the program planner who starts with a concern for emotions is not subtracting from academic priorities. In fact, the teacher will actually *increase* the likelihood that children will benefit intellectually and academically. A focus on emotions helps early childhood educators to make their entire program more effective.

Fitting in Another Curriculum

"Our early childhood curriculum already has so many new compo-nents—we have a new literacy curriculum, a mathematics curriculum, a curriculum about cultural diversity, and a technology curriculum. When would I have time to teach a curriculum on emotions?"

This, too, is an understandable concern. Many teachers are required to implement special subject-area curricula. However, the description of Natalie's program should reassure teachers that the emotion-centered cur-riculum is not a burdensome addition to existing programs. Some curricula for social and emotional learning are organized around teacher-planned units on feelings, or they schedule a period each day to address emotional issues in classroom meetings. If well-evaluated and developmentally ap-propriate (see Appendix B), these programs can be effective as part of a more comprehensive approach (Raver, 2002), in which a concern for emotional issues permeates and supports every aspect of the program. As I will show, an emotion-centered perspective can inform and enhance existing curricula in language and literacy, mathematics, science, social studies, and the arts. This perspective helps teachers decide whether existing standards and curriculum guidelines are appropriate and effective. An emotion-centered perspective may also suggest ideas for modifying these guidelines to in-crease children's engagement in the curriculum content and to enhance their acquisition of important concepts and skills.

Overemphasis on Self-Expression

"Doesn't this emphasis on emotions encourage children to express their feelings without any restrictions? My children need to learn to *control* their feelings, not to let them out."

It is easy to see why teachers might worry about this. Those who lived through misinterpretations of progressive education, open classrooms, or "free schools" may be especially hesitant to endorse a renewed emphasis on emotions. However, adopting an emotion-centered curriculum in no way requires teachers to allow unbridled expressions of feeling. In fact, cultur-ally and developmentally appropriate self-regulation of emotion, and learn-ing to understand and respond to others' feelings are important goals in young children's development. Children do not gain these abilities auto-matically. To achieve appropriate emotional control and emotional aware-ness, young children require many opportunities to observe adult models, a secure base of relationships with others, and loving guidance as they try out their emerging skills in many contexts. Like Natalie, other emotion-centered teachers let children know that their feelings are accepted. At the same time, these teachers continually guide children toward age-appropriate, culturally valued ways of expressing those feelings.

Denial of Teachers' Individual Styles

"I'm not one of those 'touchy-feely' types—I've never been comfortable telling children how I feel about everything or fawning all over them whenever they have a problem."

Being an emotion-centered teacher does not mean adopting a new or artificial style. Just as children have distinctive styles of expressing their feelings, so do their teachers. One teacher may have a lively and open expressive style, displaying positive and negative feelings directly. Another teacher has a lower key style, with muted, subtle expressions. Still another teacher may be open in expressing just some emotions—joy, for example, but not anger or sadness; or she may express emotions only in the context of program activities and not reveal her personal feelings to the children. Culture, family environment, temperament, and personal belief systems (Hyson & Lee, 1996; Hyson & Molinaro, 2001) may influence the early childhood teacher's personal emotional style.

Are all of these variations in adults' emotional styles acceptable and helpful in teaching young children? Not really. Children's play becomes disorganized when they are exposed to extreme displays of adult anger, and the children of chronically sad or depressed parents have difficulties in expressing their own feelings (Denham, 1998). Teachers' high levels of anger or depression will no doubt have similar effects. Except for these extremes, though, children can probably benefit from varied models of emotional expression.

Being emotion-centered does not mean overwhelming children with solicitude and misplaced love. Natalie and other emotion-centered teachers are careful to give children room to struggle with problems on their own, while being ready to scaffold their efforts. "This is hard for you, huh, Thomas?" Natalie says with warm concern, as Thomas struggles to push up his sleeves. Later, as Aaron walks out of the bathroom with his striped shirt just covering his bare bottom, Natalie casually comments, "Did you need some new pants, Aaron? Did you have a little bit of an accident? Do you need some help with the pants or are you all right?" When teachers maintain this sensitive balance of autonomy and support, they create conditions that promote both intellectual and emotional competence.

PROFESSIONAL GUIDELINES AND EMOTION-CENTERED PROGRAMS

An emotion-centered curriculum is consistent with a number of trends in early childhood curriculum, assessment, and teaching practices, including curriculum in several specific content areas.

Standards, Assessment, and Accountability

Federal and state governments as well as professional organizations are developing standards or expectations for child outcomes—not only for K–12 education, but also for Head Start and state prekindergarten programs, and as voluntary guidelines for state child care programs. Some of these documents now include an emphasis on emotion-related outcomes (see Resource Notes 1.2 and 1.3). An emotion-centered curriculum can help programs meet those standards, but even if standards do not specifically

---

**RESOURCE NOTE 1.2 The Standards Movement
and Early Emotional Development**

States and professional organizations are defining standards or expected learning outcomes for young children. Will these standards support or undermine a focus on emotions?

• SERVE (one of the U.S. Department of Education's regional educational laboratories: http//www.serve.org) has conducted a national survey of states' efforts to develop early childhood standards (2002). Results show that, of the 29 states that had developed standards for children below kindergarten age, 19 included social-emotional outcomes in those standards, although all include language/literacy.

• The National Association for the Education of Young Children (NAEYC) and the National Association of Early Childhood Specialists in State Departments of Education (NAECS/SDE) have published a joint position statement, *Early Learning Standards: Creating the Conditions for Success* (NAEYC & NAECS/SDE, 2002). Among the position statement's recommendations is that early childhood standards should include attention to all domains of development and learning, including emotional and social outcomes, as well as the connections among those domains. "Because research has emphasized how powerfully early social and emotional competence predict later success, and because we know that good early environments help build this competence, this domain should be given special attention in early learning standards" (p. 8).

• Head Start has published a Child Outcomes Framework (Head Start Bureau, 2001) as part of its Head Start performance standards. The Framework—intended to describe "building blocks that are important for school success"—was developed with the help of a technical work group and included a review of documents from state and professional organizations on assessment and program accountability. One of the Framework's eight domains is "Social and Emotional Development," with elements including self-concept, self-control, cooperation, social relationships, and knowledge of families and communities. Another domain, "Approaches to Learning," also includes emotion-related content: initiative and curiosity, engagement and persistence, and reasoning and problem solving (http://www.headstartinfo.org/publications/hsbulletin70/hsb70_15.htm). Appendix C shows how sections of this book may help Head Start staff support children's development in these domains.

RESOURCE NOTE 1.3 What Do State Standards Say About Emotions?

Some states are incorporating attention to emotions into their early learning standards, although many still ignore this important area, or limit social and emotional standards to expectations for appropriate classroom behavior. In contrast, here are four promising examples:

California

California's Desired Results system (*http://www.cde.ca.gov/cyfsbranch/child_development/DR2.htm*) describes "conditions of well-being" for children and families. The six desired results can be stated simply:

- Children are personally and socially competent.
- Children are effective learners.
- Children show physical and motor competence.
- Children are safe and healthy.
- Families support their children's learning and development.
- Families achieve their goals.

The first two of these Desired Results seem most closely related to early emotional development. However, California explicitly integrates all four developmental domains—cognitive, social-emotional, language, and physical development—throughout the indicators related to all six Desired Results. California's PreK Learning and Development Guidelines also place strong emphasis on the social and emotional foundations of early learning.

Connecticut

Connecticut's *Preschool Curricular Goals and Benchmarks* (State of Connecticut, State Board of Education, 1999; *http://www.state.ct.us/sde/deps/early/Frmwrkbench.pdf*) includes a set of goals and benchmarks in the area of Personal and Social Development. Like Illinois's standards, Connecticut's Guiding Principles emphasize the interrelatedness of the socio-emotional and cognitive domains. The content standards for Personal and Social Development include emotion-focused expectations such as these:

- Exhibit curiosity, creativity, self-direction, and persistence in learning situations
- Demonstrate awareness of one's own and others' feelings
- Exhibit self-control in group situations
- Use age-appropriate conflict-resolution strategies

Illinois

Like Connecticut, Illinois's Early Learning Standards (*http://www.illinoisearlylearning.org/standards/*) begin with Guiding Principles that emphasize the interconnected nature of

(continued)

RESOURCE NOTE 1.3 (*continued*)

early development and learning. Social and emotional development is included as one of eight Learning Areas; the state standards in this area are:

- Develop a positive self-concept
- Perform effectively as an individual
- Perform effectively as a member of a group
- Early childhood benchmarks related to these standards include demonstrating eagerness and curiosity as a learner; communicating needs, wants, and feelings appropriately; showing empathy and caring for others; and developing relationships with other children and adults.

Maryland

Maryland's Model for School Readiness (Maryland State Department of Education, 2001; *http://www.mdk12.org/instruction/ensure/MMSR/MMSR_Planning_Guide.pdf*) includes three outcomes in the category of Emotional Functioning:

- Attempts new experiences independently (as seen, for example, in showing eagerness and curiosity as a learner)
- Uses coping skills independently (as seen, for example, in seeking adult help when needed to resolve conflicts)
- Perseveres in activities independently (as seen, for example, in sustaining attention over time, even when encountering problems)

describe emotional outcomes, attention to emotions will increase children's ability to be successful in other, more academic domains.

Developmentally Appropriate Practices and Early Childhood Program Standards

NAEYC's guidelines for developmentally appropriate practices (Bredekamp & Copple, 1997), as well as NAEYC's early childhood program accreditation criteria (1998), emphasize that adults should respond to young children's interests and emotional needs in a warm, sensitive manner. These guidelines and criteria also call for varied, flexible teaching styles that support children's self-esteem and build confidence, security, and positive feelings about learning. Finally, NAEYC's guidelines emphasize the importance of attending to, and actively promoting, all areas of young children's development, including emotional development. As NAEYC's standards for accredited early childhood programs are revised and implemented, the research base for these and other recommendations will be even more explicit and elaborated.

Reaching Potentials: Appropriate Curriculum and Assessment for Young Children (Bredekamp & Rosegrant, 1992) extends NAEYC's focus on developmentally appropriate practices into a more specific discussion of appropriate curriculum content for young children. Curriculum content must be *meaningful* in order to be both developmentally appropriate and educationally worthwhile. Inevitably, curriculum that is meaningful to young children is linked to emotionally significant people and events. When curriculum is meaningful, children set their own goals and feel the satisfaction of exploring problems and discovering solutions. Eleanor Duckworth's (1987) phrase "the having of wonderful ideas" captures the affective-cognitive integration of a meaningful, emotion-centered curriculum. Ideas are wonderful to children when they "have" the ideas through repeated learning cycles of *awareness*, *exploration*, *inquiry*, and *application* (Bredekamp & Rosegrant, 1992). Curiosity, focused attention, surprise, and joy accompany this learning process; children may also experience sadness, anger, and even fear as they tackle problems alone or with others. Encountering and coping with *all* of these feelings provides a rich context for early learning.

Language, Literacy, and Emotional Development

One of the most significant developments in recent years has been a new focus on early language and literacy development (Neuman & Dickinson, 2001; Neuman, Copple, & Bredekamp, 2001; Snow, Burns, & Griffin, 1999). Spurred by concerns about the large number of children whose academic futures are in jeopardy because of reading difficulties, federal and state governments and professional associations have given research-based language and literacy instruction a high priority. Whatever the methods, most writers agree that reading and writing must be linked to personally meaningful, emotionally powerful experiences (Davidson, 1996; Owocki, 1999, 2001). Successful early literacy programs emphasize phonemic awareness and other foundational skills, while also encouraging children to talk and write about personally relevant matters. In these programs children may create their own books—encouraging pride and joy—and children read and are told stories that address emotionally significant matters. These activities not only create interest today, but they also build motivation for tomorrow's readers and writers (Guthrie & Wigfield, 2000).

Effective language and literacy programs for young children also stress the warm interpersonal context of early literacy experiences. When children cuddle on soft pillows as they read with their friends or their teachers, or when caregivers hold toddlers as they look at and talk about books, children receive far more than physical comfort. The emotional power of these warm settings can strengthen children's disposition to use language and to love books and reading. An explicit focus on emotions should strengthen literacy learning rather than detracting from it.

Mathematics, Science, and Emotions

As with literacy, a series of national reports have recommended improvements in mathematics and science education (Glenn Commission, 2000; Kilpatrick, Swafford, & Findell, 2001; National Council of Teachers of Mathematics [NCTM], 2002). NAEYC and NCTM (2002) have published a joint position statement on early mathematical learning and "what it takes" to ensure that all children are able to experience excellent mathematics instruction. These recommendations emphasize that mathematics and science must be personally and socially meaningful to children. The title of a popular early childhood curriculum guide, *Mathematics Their Way* (Baratta-Lorton, 1994), reflects the belief that mathematics will be understood and used by children when it builds on their enthusiasms, interests, and natural curiosity. This book and many other guides to early mathematics and science education (e.g., Andrews & Trafton, 2002; Chaille & Britain, 1997; Copley, 1999, 2000; Kamii, 2000; Seefeldt & Galper, 2002) emphasize the use of familiar, personally relevant materials and situations, encouraging teachers to give children the excitement of discovery and the emotional satisfaction of meeting self-selected challenges.

Experts in child development and curriculum recommend placing academic content—including mathematical and scientific learning—within a social context (e.g., Berk & Winsler, 1995; DeVries, Zan, Hildebrandt, Edmiaston, & Sales, 2002; Helm & Beneke, 2003). Children are encouraged to work in cooperative groups, sharing ideas and expertise. This social context also includes the family; in many early childhood mathematics programs, homework brings parents and young children together to describe, count, classify, or identify mathematical relationships in home and neighborhood events (Coates & Stenmark, 1997).

Emotions, the Project Approach, and Reggio Emilia

Many educators recommend that the early childhood curriculum should be centered on projects or themes (e.g., Helm & Katz, 2001; Bredekamp & Rosegrant, 1992; Katz & Chard, 2000). These writers stress that a thematically organized curriculum should be more than a superficial collection of topics plucked out of a resource book. Rather, project work is an intellectually challenging activity that grows out of children's deeply felt interests and allows children to gain insight into important concepts through personally constructed knowledge. Anyone who has done this kind of project work knows that children can become deeply engaged in investigations of many facets of their world. This emotional engagement sustains a remarkable level of attention and effort. Persuasive examples are the descriptions of extended project work in the Italian preschools of Reggio Emilia (Edwards, Gandini, & Forman, 1998; Project Zero & Reggio Children, 2001), the project work found in Helm's and Katz's publications, and the yearlong "penguin project" described in Ayers's book, *The Good Preschool Teacher* (1989). For this level of involvement to occur, teachers must invest the topic—whatever it is—with emotional significance, and they must be able to stimulate and sustain children's engagement.

Emotions and a Curriculum That Honors Diversity

As we await the increasingly diverse "Children of 2010" (Andrews & Washington, 1998), many early childhood educators are even more committed to an inclusive, multicultural or antibias approach to curriculum, as articulated in NAEYC's position statement on linguistic and cultural diversity (NAEYC, 1995) and in work such as that of the Early Childhood Equity Alliance (2002) and other advocates for a curriculum that honors diversity (Copple, 2003; Derman-Sparks & A.B.C. Task Force, 1989; Ramsey, 1998). These writers urge early childhood educators to take an active role in countering prejudice and bias related to gender, language, ethnicity, religious affiliation, disability, and other human characteristics. This approach explicitly rejects the "tourist curriculum" (a week's unit on Japan, a Hanukkah party, and so on). Instead, proponents of inclusive, multicultural, or antibias curricula favor an integrated approach that builds positive images, challenges young children's stereotypes, offers children tools for change, and addresses issues of exclusion and inclusion in age-appropriate contexts.

This brief description should show that an inclusive or antibias approach is fully compatible with an emotion-centered curriculum. Awareness of children's emotional responses to exclusion, bias, and difference helps early childhood practitioners to select appropriate classroom strategies, monitor their impact, and adapt curriculum to individual needs (Copple, 2003). An inclusive or antibias curriculum requires an affectively based approach to issues of fairness and equity, stressing empathy and emotional as well as intellectual engagement.

REFOCUSING ON EMOTIONS

For most early childhood professionals, building an emotion-centered curriculum will not mean starting from scratch. Rather, it will involve *refocusing*, to place greater, more thoughtful emphasis on emotions; to integrate emotional concerns more fully across the curriculum; and to consider emotion-related criteria in developing standards, curriculum goals, content, teaching strategies, and assessment practices (NAEYC & NAECS/SDE, 2003). Families are integral partners in this process; Resource Note 1.4 offers suggestions for effective communication with families about emotion-related issues.

The process of curriculum development is—or should be—highly individual. Every practitioner, or every team of practitioners, has different

---

RESOURCE NOTE 1.4 Talking With Families About Emotions

Many early childhood teachers find it easier to talk with parents about literacy and mathematics than about more personally or emotionally charged topics (Olson & Hyson, 2003). Conversations about children's emotional development—especially if concerns exist—may touch upon sensitive issues of family adversity, child rearing practices, or cultural values. Yet children's emotional competence is best supported when teachers and families work together (Parlakian & Seibel, 2002). To create good conversations about emotions:

- Establish a foundation for communication through a respectful, reciprocal relationship with every family.
- Build on families' unique strengths to help them create the kind of supportive relationships with their children that nurture emotional security and mental health.
- Observe and appreciate each child's unique emotional style, using one or more of the observation and assessment tools described in this book.
- Share your goals for children's emotional development with families, and learn more about their goals.
- Make discussions of children's progress toward emotional competence an integral part of parent conferences.
- Enter emotionally difficult territory (such as sharing a serious concern) by beginning with the positive and learning more about the parent's own perceptions and possible concerns. "Advice" is less important than shared ideas about how to address problems together.

References

Olson, M., & Hyson, M. (2003). Supporting teachers, strengthening families: A new NAEYC initiative. *Young Children, 58*(3), 74–75.
Parlakian, R., & Seibel, N.L. (2002). *Building strong foundations.* Washington, DC: Zero to Three.

---

personal, emotional, and professional reasons for undertaking an emotional refocusing. Whatever the reasons, the refocusing process requires reflection upon, and decisions about, three topics: goals and standards, content and teaching practices, and assessment practices.

Selecting Goals

The refocusing practitioner or staff might begin by reviewing the program's existing or proposed goals, as well as program-level, agency, state, or professional association standards (refer to Resource Notes 1.2 and 1.3). In looking at these goals or standards, staff might ask three questions:

1. Are the program's goals, standards, or desired child outcomes fundamentally compatible with an emotion-centered approach?

2. Do these goals adequately support children's emotional development?

3. Do those goals that are "nonemotional" (such as academic skill standards) provide room for emotions to be integrated with other goals?

If an existing set of goals (either a comprehensive set for a whole early childhood program or standards related to a specific content area) shows that emotions are not adequately represented, Saarni's (1999) description of the components of "emotional competence" may give additional help to the program planner. Resource Note 1.5 presents a summary of these components.

Reexamining Content and Teaching Practices

Refocusing on emotions also means examining existing curriculum content and teaching practices to ensure that they contain rich opportunities for children to develop emotional competence and link emotions to learning. The chapters that follow will provide many examples. Exactly how this

---

RESOURCE NOTE 1.5 Components of Emotional Competence

1. Awareness of one's own emotional state, including the possibility that one is experiencing multiple emotions
2. Ability to discern others' emotions, based on cues in the situation and in people's expressive behavior
3. Ability to use the vocabulary of emotion and expressive terms common in one's culture or subculture
4. Capacity for empathic and sympathetic involvement in others' emotional experiences
5. Ability to realize that inner emotional states do not necessarily correspond to outer expression of feelings, in oneself or in others
6. Capacity for adaptive coping with unpleasant or distressing emotions by using self-regulatory strategies that alleviate the intensity or duration of these feelings
7. Awareness that close personal relationships are partly defined by how emotions are communicated within the relationship
8. Capacity for emotional self-efficacy: The person views her- or himself as feeling, overall, the way she or he wants to feel

Note. This list includes some competencies that require a high level of cognitive and socioemotional maturity. Nevertheless, the competencies are often present in earlier forms among young children and may help early childhood programs develop long-term goals. From *The Development of Emotional Competence* (p. 5) by C. Saarni, 1999, New York: Guilford Press. Adapted with permission.

curriculum review happens will depend on the professional setting in which teachers work and the program's current state of curriculum development.

For example, perhaps a team of primary grade teachers is reviewing an already adopted mathematics curriculum. Focusing on the content and recommended implementation strategies from an emotion-centered perspective, they might decide that children would benefit from sharing their work with their families as a way of building pride and confidence. Therefore, the teachers might decide to add a "family night" to a planned unit on measurement, and they might plan to build several activities around measuring objects at home, enlisting the help of family members. The team might also find that creating a cozy mathematics corner with pillows, math-related books and puzzles, and other problem-solving materials could foster a sense of comfort and security and a more sociable environment than when children are seated at formica-topped tables. They might consider increasing the "laughter quotient" in the mathematics program by posting a math joke or math riddle of the day. The teaching team might also consider strategies to deal with the inevitable frustration some children may experience as they tackle the new materials, with the goal both of maximizing children's success and of using the mathematics curriculum to build children's capacity to deal with their own negative emotional states.

Using vignettes from a number of high-quality early childhood programs, the next six chapters will offer many examples of how emotional refocusing can help teachers and children get the most out of the early childhood curriculum.

Analyzing Assessment Practices

Assessment practices in early childhood programs have been closely scrutinized in recent years. In addition to their limited ability to document children's progress, many current assessment practices have been accused of undermining children's self-confidence and creating negative feelings about learning. However, assessment of children's progress need not have harmful emotional consequences. In fact, good assessment practices can support development and learning in all domains and increase children's feelings of engagement and satisfaction.

Descriptions of effective, research-based approaches to early childhood assessment (McAfee & Leong, 2002; Meisels & Atkins-Burnett, 2002) appear well suited to an emotion-centered curriculum. In such a program, teachers need to be sure assessments are conducted in a positive emotional climate, minimizing children's fear, distress, and sadness. Collecting work samples (Meisels, Liaw, Dorfman, & Nelson, 1995), using visual documentation (Helm, Beneke, & Steinheimer, 1997), developing portfolios (Grace & Shores, 1994), and conferencing with children about their activities are all strategies that can support rather than undermine young children's emotional development and that can create a richly textured portrait of children's developmental progress. The results of assessment should lead to emotional as well as academic benefits for children, increasing children's feelings of pride, competence, and self-efficacy.

Besides ensuring that all assessments take place in a supportive emotional climate, teachers also need to adopt specific strategies to assess the emotion-related aspects of children's progress. To do this, teachers must assess children's *feelings* about curriculum content and their *dispositions* related to learning (e.g., curiosity, initiative, and tolerance for frustration) as well as their mastery of skills and concepts.

Teachers in an emotion-centered program will also implement procedures for continuously assessing children's emotional competence, using knowledge about typical developmental characteristics as well as information about individual children's culture, temperament, and family context. Although many more tools are available than in the past, there is still no simple checklist that will tell the practitioner everything she or he wants to know—and perhaps that is just as well. Good assessment always relies on multiple sources of information. Appendix D lists some promising assessment tools that teachers might use to understand children better, to plan the program, and to communicate with other practitioners.

Moving toward an emotion-focused curriculum is a developmental journey. Where a program is right now is less important than where it is headed. Resource Note 1.6 offers a guide for staff to track their progress.

RESOURCE NOTE 1.6 Focusing on Emotions in Early Childhood Programs: Where Are You on the Journey?

Choosing Emotion-Focused Goals

From: Haven't begun to consider
To: Reviewing our program goals in light of research on emotions
To: Using a team approach to revise and recommit to emotion-focused goals

Reexamining Content and Teaching Practices

From: Haven't begun to reexamine
To: Bringing staff together to analyze current curriculum and teaching practices in light of emotions research and emotion-focused goals
To: Incorporating an emotions focus into many aspects of curriculum and teaching

Analyzing Assessment Practices

From: Haven't begun to analyze from an emotions perspective
To: Considering existing assessments for their impact on children's feelings and for their ability to derive good information about children's emotional development
To: Revising the program's assessment systems to support the overall emotional focus of the program, adopting new assessment tools as needed

CONCLUSION

Beginning with a description of Natalie's program for 2-year-olds, this chapter has outlined the central features of an emotion-centered early childhood curriculum. It has also addressed some concerns practitioners may have about this approach to early childhood education. While acknowledging these concerns, I have emphasized that a focus on emotions can support every curriculum area, every area of development, and every dimension of school readiness. The chapter has offered suggestions on how to begin the process of "emotional refocusing," suggesting careful attention to program goals, curriculum content, and assessment practices.

But what happens in daily life? The next six chapters will describe effective strategies to construct an emotion-focused program (see Resource Note 1.7). Four of the early childhood practitioners who were introduced earlier— Hope, Terry, Christine, and Denise—will be featured in these chapters. In Chapter 2, we will focus on the first, most basic goal of an emotion-focused program: creating a secure emotional environment. We will begin by seeing how Hope approaches this task with her class of primary-grade children.

RESOURCE NOTE 1.7 The Goals of an Emotion-Focused Early Childhood Program

Research and professional guidelines have identified these six goals as especially important for children's current and future development.

1. Creating a secure emotional environment
If teachers create an emotionally secure climate, children are able to explore and learn.
2. Helping children understand emotions
If teachers promote emotional understanding, children have insight into their own and others' feelings, becoming more empathic and socially competent.
3. Modeling genuine, appropriate emotional responses
If teachers themselves show real emotions, and if they are effective models, children are likely to adopt appropriate ways of showing their feelings.
4. Supporting children's regulation of emotions
If teachers gradually guide children toward self-regulation, children will gain powerful tools that lead to healthy development in multiple domains.
5. Recognizing and honoring children's expressive styles
If teachers respect individual differences in emotional expressiveness, while promoting culturally and developmentally appropriate expression, children can move forward within a supportive environment.
6. Uniting children's learning with positive emotions
If teachers give children many opportunities to experience the joys and overcome the frustrations of new learning experiences, they become able to tackle hard work, persist at tasks, and seek out challenges.

Chapter 2

Creating a Secure Emotional Environment

The children in Hope's multiage primary class are huddled in small groups, working intently at deciphering some printed "job application" forms. The class is preparing for an open house to be held that evening. Today they will make sandwiches and Jell-O treats in an assembly-line food factory and make signs advertising their café. Tonight parents and other family members can buy snacks at the café.

Hope has created forms on which are listed various jobs and their requirements, as developed in class meetings: "Sandwich maker: Must be clean, know how to use a plastic knife, know how to make sandwiches." "Label maker: Must have neat printing, be careful worker, like to write." Under each job, there is space for children to write their name, age, and qualifications for the job. Earlier, Hope had assigned the children to small groups, mixing ages and reading skills. Before the children began the task, Hope told them to think about the things they know how to do and like to do and see which jobs have requirements that fit their skills. Now each group has found a comfortable spot to meet. One group is in the book area, furnished with soft cushions and large stuffed animals. Another group settled in behind the easels, pulling chairs into a circle. They work together to read the job descriptions and to decide which jobs they would like to apply for.

"I can 'carry' and add," Serena announces to her group, looking at the requirements for Banker. "I make sandwiches real good at home," Xavier declares. Mario comes up to a visitor, holding out the form. "I can't read that word," he says matter-of-factly, pointing at *organized*. After he figures it out with help, he rejoins the group and tells them what it is.

Each group approaches the task in its own way. In some groups, one child is clearly in charge. Seven-year-old Eileen directs each child in her group to take turns reading. In another group, Serena reads to the rest of the children, holding up the application as she points to the words. While the children work, Hope walks around, reminding them to "think about what things you are good at," helping with hard words, and listening with interest to children's descriptions of their experiences in sandwich making, money handling, and writing.

"You have to be *very delicate* when you cut Jell-O Jigglers," Amanda patiently explains to one of the younger children. "If you mess up with the cutter, the Jell-O gets all smooshed. Do you think you can be very delicate?" Corey nods solemnly. "Then you could apply for that," Amanda pronounces.

The classroom community experienced by Hope's children embodies all the characteristics of a secure emotional environment. Without this foundation, an emotion-focused curriculum would be impossible to achieve. In this chapter, I will examine evidence that emotional security is the foundation of healthy personalities, pointing out that social and economic disintegration is placing young children's feelings of security at ever-increasing risk. I will describe some specific ways that early childhood teachers can build an environment of predictability, acceptance, and responsiveness. The chapter will recommend a variety of security-building, affective communication processes, including smiles, gazes, touches, and words, while emphasizing the need for cultural, developmental, and individual sensitivity. Finally, we will reflect on how transitions and new challenges may influence children's security needs as the year progresses, and how emotion-centered teachers can meet those needs in flexible, appropriate ways.

EMOTIONAL SECURITY AND THE HEALTHY PERSONALITY

The Importance of Security

Feelings of security are the basic ingredient of a healthy personality. Many clinicians, researchers, and developmental theorists have attested to the importance of emotional security.

Erik Erikson (1950, 1959) is one of the theorists whose work is discussed later in this book in Exploration 1. Erikson described a sense of trust as the first accomplishment of infancy. Through repeated experiences, most babies learn that adults can generally be relied on to meet their needs and to provide love and admiration. If this healthy balance of "trust versus mistrust" is not achieved during the first year of life, later development will be difficult. However, later experiences (including those provided by high-quality early childhood programs) can offer new opportunities to strengthen a child's sense of trust.

Bowlby (1998), Mahler (Mahler, Pine, & Bergman, 2000), and Ainsworth (Ainsworth, Blehar, Waters, & Wall, 1978) established the importance of a "secure base" in early childhood. When children feel they can count on important, loved people to provide comfort, they have a strong foundation of confidence that allows them to explore their surroundings. This exploration may take many forms, including the first tentative steps of the toddler (who then staggers back to his caregiver's embrace), the 3-year-old's friendship overtures with unfamiliar children, and the first grader's struggle with a new book. Although the ways in which children show "secure base behavior" differ across cultures (Posada, Gao, Wu, & Posada, 1995), the need for a secure base seems universal.

Risks to Security

Early childhood classrooms have always included a certain number of children whose emotional security was fragile. However, in years past, early childhood teachers observed that most children entered their care with a well-established sense of trust, emotional security, and psychological safety. These children simply needed the teacher's help to extend an already existing secure base, transferring feelings of affection and trust from family to other caregivers and, in time, to peers.

Today this task no longer seems so simple—if it ever really was. More and more children arrive in child care, Head Start, prekindergarten, or kindergarten with a history of inconsistent, shifting care arrangements, which may have included multiple foster placements or a rapid turnover of caregivers. Parents whose own early environments were insecure may have treated their children in unresponsive, neglectful, and even abusive ways. Seeing rage and violence at home or in their neighborhoods, children come to the early childhood program with little confidence that their world is safe, predictable, or helpful. Even children from stable families sometimes feel that they stand on emotionally shaky ground because their parents seem to value them only for their academic performances and their adherence to adult standards.

The process of attachment and the formation of secure attachments have received decades of study (Cassidy & Shaver, 1999). Many studies have shown that insecurely attached children—those with anxious–ambivalent/ resistant, anxious-avoidant, and disorganized attachment relationships with their parents or other caregivers—are likely to have later problems with their own relationships (Honig, 2002). Exploration 3 in Part II provides a further look at this and other influences. During preschool, children with insecure attachment histories may show lower self-esteem, and they are often extremely dependent or extremely disruptive. At all ages, people whose early relationships have left them with insecure attachments seem to have a hard time finding a healthy balance of emotional self-regulation. Many either avoid negative emotions or express anger in uncontrolled, inappropriate ways (Bell, 1998). Besides children who are insecurely attached, some writers (e.g., Chisholm, 1998; Zeanah, Boris, & Lieberman, 2000) have also described "nonattached" children who have not had any consistent caregiver and who therefore have had no opportunity to develop selective attachments. These children, too, are at developmental risk.

Investing in Secure Relationships

For all these reasons, the task of creating a secure emotional environment within the early childhood program is more important than ever (Honig, 2002; Howes & Ritchie, 2002; Shonkoff & Phillips, 2001). It is also more difficult. The same children who lack a foundation of emotional security are often the targets of further criticism and harsh treatment in early childhood programs, because teachers and peers react negatively to their inappropriate behavior. This cycle further undermines their feelings of security and decreases their ability to benefit from intellectual and social opportunities.

Early childhood teachers are in a position to support children's emotional security by building strong, reciprocal, and respectful relationships with their families. Parents who feel isolated and under stress may find it hard to establish nurturing relationships with their young children; support and communication from teachers helps create positive bonds and reduces the risk of harm to children (Olson & Hyson, 2003).

Despite these efforts, many children continue to experience insecure family environments. Emotionally positive relationships with teachers can go a long way toward building resilience, even for maltreated children (Pianta, 1992, 1999; Pianta, La Paro, Payne, Cox & Bradley, 2002). High-quality infant-toddler programs base the entire curriculum on relationships (Program for Infant-Toddler Caregivers, 2000; Zero to Three, 1992). The benefits are clear: Children who had close, secure relationships with their child care teachers also had better relationships with other children (Elicker & Fortner-Wood, 1995). And 5 years later, children who had close relationships with teachers in the preschool years were still rated high in social competence and high in child-teacher relationships (Howes, 2000). Building these relationships is a wise investment (see Resource Note 2.1).

BUILDING SECURITY THROUGH PROGRAM ENVIRONMENTS

Young children have several basic needs that must be met if they are to develop or reconstruct a feeling of emotional security. First, they require an environment that is *predictable*. A predictable environment builds security by letting children know how people are likely to behave and how events are likely to unfold. Second, children will feel emotionally secure in an environment that is *warmly accepting* of who they are and what they think and feel. Third, children require an environment that is *responsive*. A responsive environment shows children that they matter, that their actions have consequences and can make a difference in what happens in their world. An emotion-centered early childhood program deliberately sets out to meet these needs (see Resource Note 2.2).

RESOURCE NOTE 2.1 Recent Research on the Value
of Secure Relationships: Neurons to Neighborhoods

The National Research Council's report, *From Neurons to Neighborhoods: The Science of Early Childhood Development* (Shonkoff & Phillips, 2001), puts secure adult-child relationships at the center of positive development.

An expert panel reviewed and synthesized the extensive body of scientific research on early attachment, security, and later development. Several quotes reflect the panel's consensus:

- "Children grow and thrive in the context of close and dependable relationships that provide love and nurturance, security, responsive interaction, and encouragement and exploration" (p. 389).
- "The astonishing developmental achievements of the earliest years occur naturally when parents and other caregivers talk, read, and play with young children and respond sensitively to their cues" (p. 412).
- "Not surprisingly, the basic elements of high-quality care closely resemble the qualities of good parenting. Children's basic needs for consistent, sensitive, and stimulating care transcend the difference between home and child care" (p. 326).
- "Nurturing, stable, consistent relationships are the key to healthy growth, development, and learning." (p. 412).

RESOURCE NOTE 2.2 Building Security: Early Childhood Educators'
Role in Child Abuse Prevention

For young children, emotional security is grounded in their families and their early childhood programs, working together as partners. Yet this partnership can be challenging to
teachers and to families. In 2002, NAEYC embarked on a national initiative—*Supporting
Teachers, Strengthening Families*—to help early childhood educators prevent child abuse
and neglect and promote children's secure, healthy social and emotional development.
Because of their relationships with families and their ability to support families of young
children, early childhood educators are in a unique position to meet these goals. The
Doris Duke Charitable Foundation (DDCF) generously supported this work.

With the foundation's support, *Supporting Teachers, Strengthening Families:*

- Conducted a national study of almost 2000 early childhood professionals
- Sent out a strong message about how early childhood professionals and family
  members can work together to promote young children's development and
  prevent harm to children.
- Developed resources and materials to help early childhood professionals prevent harm to children, build positive family relationships and communication,
  and ensure healthy development.

Supporting Teachers, Strengthening Families is based on NAEYC's position statement
*Prevention of Child Abuse in Early Childhood Programs and the Responsibilities of Early Child-
hood Professionals to Prevent Child Abuse* (NAEYC, 1996) and other important NAEYC resources that describe early childhood educators' legal and ethical responsibilities and underscore
the importance of respectful, reciprocal relationships with families in preventing child abuse
and neglect and promoting children's secure, healthy, social and emotional development.

Learn more about *Supporting Teachers, Strengthening Families* from Olson and Hyson
(2003) online at *www.naeyc.org.*

Predictability

Hope's multiage classroom is much more flexible in its schedule and
style than many other first- or second-grade programs. The foundation of
predictability that Hope has built allows the children to function comfortably within this setting. Arriving on a Monday morning, a visitor would
see the group deciding who will take responsibility for various classroom
jobs, including General Inspector, Library Helper, Table Washers, and Writing Inspectors. Different children volunteer for these jobs each week, but
the structure of this routine provides a secure base.

A predictable physical environment also provides emotional security to children. Children derive pleasure and comfort from knowing where
things are and from having personal space for loved possessions. There are
important reasons to have cubbies for children, to have a special shelf for

in-progress art projects, or to have a "treasure basket" where personal items can be deposited until it is time to go home. These reasons go beyond classroom order and cleanliness. They speak powerfully to children, letting them know that this environment is one they can depend on.

Acceptance

Hope has also created a program permeated with acceptance. Part of the climate of acceptance comes simply from Hope's attitude. As she greets children and as she talks with them about their lives, her manner conveys sincere enjoyment. Children clearly feel that their ideas and personal stories will be appreciatively welcomed. "Mrs. Connor," Maria shyly injected during a group discussion about parents' night, "My aunt saw my picture in the post office" (a local newspaper had carried a story about Hope's class). "Was she excited to see it?" Hope responded, leaning forward with interest. Maria nodded vigorously, and the discussion turned back to jobs for the food factory.

Acceptance is also reflected in the early childhood program's physical environment. Hope's classroom, like others with emotion-centered programs, celebrates children's out-of-school experiences. Photographs and drawings of the children's families, homes, and pets; stories about familiar events and people; familiar, culturally valued objects—all of these surround children with a comfortable blanket of security as they tackle the new challenges of child care, Head Start, or first grade.

In the accepting early childhood program, children's mistakes are treated matter-of-factly. Mistakes are not signs of inadequacy. "Did you find the mistake you made? Good!" Hope commented to Rachel. Because of this attitude, children readily admit their mistakes to Hope and to other children. "I lost count because of the door closing," Carlo admitted after the tambourine exercise. Later on, Nicholas stated, "I don't know what to do," pointing at the job application form. "I can help Nicholas, Mrs. Connor," said Eric, moving his chair closer to his friend.

Mistakes can also be fixed. Serena worked diligently to create a sign for the café. First she lettered *SUPER GOOD FAST FOOD* on a large sheet of paper, using large block letters. Then she began to paint the letters "in a pattern," as she said, with three different colors. She lost control of the brush and made a small green streak in the wrong place. "I messed up," she confessed to Hope. "You know what grown-ups do when they make a mistake?" Hope said. "They use White Out to fix it. I have some right here, and you can use it after the painting dries."

Hope's multiage primary class includes typical variations in temperament and learning style, together with an unusually wide range of ages and skill levels. Hope's program is organized so that these variations become strengths, not problems. While conveying confidence that children will develop additional competencies over time and with practice, Hope also helps children feel accepted right now, with the skills they have. The weekly job lists and projects like the food factory show children that many skills and interests are needed for big jobs to get done. "Serena, you know a lot about that. You will be a very important person in the food factory. When we have a problem with making the signs, we can go to Serena."

Responsiveness

Hope's program illustrates the value of responsiveness in establishing emotional security. Children feel they can have an effect on their environment. The walls of the room are covered with signs and pictures that the children have made; the shelves contain class-made books. Many decisions in the café project have been made by the children, including what to sell, where to post signs, and what the signs should say.

After the morning's work, Hope gathered the group on the rug again. "I'd like to talk about our food factory experience," she explained. "We've never had a food factory before. How did you feel about it? Did you feel that you did an important job?" (It is hard to convey the sincere tone of these questions, which differs in important ways from the artificial whipping up of enthusiasm that typifies some early childhood programs.)

Heads nodded and children beamed as they looked at the cartons of baggies filled with sandwiches, crackers, and Jell-O Jigglers, each labeled with the name of the snack and the price. "Did it seem like you were working in a factory?" asked Hope. "I think I should be *paid* for something like that!" Molly vehemently declared. This opinion led to an extended discussion of how the children might "pay" themselves, with ideas ranging from eating all the food to giving everyone some money afterward.

BUILDING SECURITY THROUGH EMOTIONAL COMMUNICATION

Early childhood teachers can help build a climate of emotional security with their faces, bodies, and voices. As Resource Note 2.3 emphasizes, men *and* women make important contributions to this task. Smiles, warm gazes, physical closeness, affectionate touches, and supportive words all help children feel comfortable and accepted. However, to be most effective these avenues of communication must fit children's developmental, personal, and cultural characteristics.

Smiling and Gazing

Children feel emotionally secure when their teacher smiles warmly at them. There is a big difference, however, between smiles that are impersonally and even falsely distributed and the personal, private smile that says to a child, "I see you and you are important to me."

RESOURCE NOTE 2.3 Where Are the Men?

This book features seven teachers who are all caring and competent—and who all happen to be women. One might ask, "Where are the men?"

In early childhood education, men have been in short supply. Only 3% of the members of the National Association for the Education of Young Children (NAEYC) are male. Even in public schools, a mere 15% of teachers are male, and in programs for children below kindergarten the numbers are even lower. Historical traditions and gender stereotypes have contributed to this disparity.

What difference does the absence of men make, as the early childhood education field tries to support young children's emotional development? Many men and women in the field would argue that it makes a significant difference (Nelson, 2003). Beyond the importance of male role models in education, men are important contributors to nurturing young children—whether as fathers or as education professionals. Although some believe that men are not nurturing enough to support early development, research on fathers strongly refutes that belief (Lamb, 1997). Young children can develop emotionally secure attachments to men and women, looking to their fathers and other men to help them understand and express feelings.

Yet men in education are often viewed with suspicion when they try to establish the kind of emotionally close relationships young children need (Hyson, Whitehead, & Prudhoe, 1988). Many male teachers acknowledge that these public perceptions inhibit their ability to comfort and express physical affection to children (Sargent, 2001).

Bryan Nelson, director of MenTeach (www.menteach.org), emphasizes that young children need to see that men can also be caring and gentle. And yet men are not—and should not be—exactly the same as women in the ways that they teach and nurture young children. Depending on their personal style as well as gender-specific characteristics, men can complement women's approaches to supporting emotional development. Many men interact with children in more vigorous and unpredictable ways than women; men also tend to let children explore new experiences a bit more before stepping in to help (Pruett, 2001). These and other differences contribute to children's ability to establish positive relationships with a variety of important adults.

References

Hyson, M. C., Whitehead, L. C., & Prudhoe, C. (1988). Influences on attitudes toward physical affection between adults and children. *Early Childhood Research Quarterly, 3*(1), 55–75.

Lamb, M. E. (Ed.) (1997). *The role of the father in child development.* 3d ed. New York: Wiley.

Nelson, B. (2003). The importance of men teachers and reasons why there are so few: A survey of members of NAEYC. [Online: *www.menteach.org*]

Pruett, K. (2001). *Fatherneed: Why father care is as essential as mother care for your child.* New York: Broadway Books.

Sargent, P. (2001). *Real men or real teachers? Contradictions in the lives of men elementary school teachers.* Harriman, TN: Men's Studies Press.

When a teacher looks directly into a child's eyes, this usually sends the message that the adult is interested in the child's thoughts and feelings. But different cultures have different standards about eye contact between adults and children. Some children, especially those living in Asian, Latino, or Native American cultures, may have been brought up to avoid looking directly at adults as a sign of respect for their authority and status. Emotion-centered teachers need to be sensitive to these cultural norms, because children will feel *less* secure if teachers violate the customs of family and community.

Although the specific style of interaction may vary by culture, most adults naturally engage in playful turn-taking interactions with infants, reacting to the babies' expressions, sounds, and actions with immediate, spontaneous expression changes. When adults do not respond in this "contingent" kind of way, many infants are visibly disturbed: They may become physically agitated, fuss, cry, and eventually turn away helplessly.

Proximity

Simply sitting close to a child can also build security. Natalie, the teacher in Chapter 1, is constantly surrounded by children. Natalie's 2-year-olds are continually "refueling" at her side, spending most of their time close to her, and then moving off for brief forays to other parts of the room. Natalie often positions herself near an activity that she wants the children to try, knowing that they will be more likely to explore a new art material, for example, if they can do so in their teacher's comforting presence. Looking at the older children in Hope's class, one still sees evidence of this emotional refueling process as children touch base with their teacher to show her their work or whisper a confidence.

Affectionate Touch

Smiling, looking, and sitting nearby are not enough. At every age, children gain emotional security from affectionate touch.

Culture may also determine children's expectations about being held and cuddled. "Collectivist" cultures, including Puerto Rican and other Latino cultures, strongly emphasize physical closeness between parents and children, as a way of fostering interdependendence (Greenfield, 1994; Miller & Harwood, 2001). In many Korean and Chinese families, children are "babied" beyond the age that many European American teachers would feel is appropriate. Toddlers and even older preschool children from Asian cultures have generally come to expect that adults will respond to their distress by immediately picking them up, holding them, and carrying them around for long periods. Although teachers need not adopt every practice of the child's culture in order for the child to develop emotional security, the emotion-centered teacher will work closely with families to become aware of these differences, modifying interactions to provide the child with a predictable, culturally safe environment (Lynch & Hansen, 1998).

Whatever the cultural norms, not every child desires an equal dose of physical affection. Some children seem to be less "huggy" than others, even as newborns. They prefer to be held upright, viewing their surroundings, rather than being snuggled close to their caregiver's body. As they get older, these children may pull away when hugged or touched affectionately. The sensitive teacher respects these individual differences and finds other ways to build emotional security with the noncuddlers.

A few children may have had frightening experiences that color their responses to physical contact in the early childhood program. Physically abused children may shrink from any touch, fearing that it is a sign of danger, not affection. Sexually abused children may place erotic interpretations on adult touch, creating complex problems that require professional consultation (Cicchetti & Carlson, 1989).

Some periods of development may bring wide fluctuations in children's need for affectionate touch. Mahler (Mahler, Pine, & Bergman, 2000) describes how, within just a few minutes, the newly walking toddler may oscillate between two extremes: clinging to the caregiver and angrily pushing the caregiver away, wanting to "do it myself!"

Despite these fluctuations, most preschool children welcome physical affection. Some experienced preschool teachers find it difficult to make the transition to teaching older children, because primary-grade children may actively reject hugs from grown-ups. Sometimes teachers deal with children's rejection of their affectionate touches by abandoning all physical contact. Teachers who are experienced with older children find that the children do need and want physical affection, but they may prefer it with—literally—a light touch. Hope does not overwhelm her children with physical affection. Instead, she will touch a child in passing, give a quick squeeze around the shoulders, or a hand on a 7-year-old's back as he struggles with a writing task. These contacts may meet the older child's need for physical nurturance without arousing his fears of sliding into a dependent, babyish relationship with adults.

The Contribution of Words

"Do you know how to spell *fast food*? Then I think you're the woman for this job." Words can build emotional security, and Lauren's happy grin when Hope expressed confidence in her skills showed that she treasured her teacher's words.

Children blossom when adults talk to them. Adults' conversations with children certainly strengthen vocabulary and later reading skills (Dickinson & Tabors, 2002; Hart & Risley, 1999), but these conversations also have emotional benefits. Even before they can carry on a conversation, infants and toddlers revel in the sound of parents' or beloved caregivers' voices. Natalie keeps up a running commentary on her 2-year-olds' activities. Her warm, reassuring, interested tone of voice conveys security; with these very young children, the words may be less important than the sound.

In using words to build security, the emotion-centered teacher again needs to be aware of cultural variations. Not every culture emphasizes intensive, face-to-face conversations with infants and toddlers. For example, Heath (1983) described rural African American communities in which toddlers spend a great deal of time observing adults talking with each other about family and community events. The adults do not seem to consider that their conversation should be directed at the children, and yet the children's language skills—and their sense of emotional security—are strong.

With older children, teachers can use words to recognize children's accomplishments. Young readers welcome little notes from their teacher ("Hi, Rachel! I am glad you are back with us today."). Words can help children feel more secure when they have to wait for something ("I just have to finish up this job, and then I will sit and look at your book with you, Andrew.").

Security grows when teachers' words help children to link past and present experiences: "Remember when Jason brought the snake to school, Tad? That was like when you brought your guinea pig, wasn't it?" or "I remember that long walk we took up the hill in the snow. I wonder what the hill looks like now that the snow is all gone?" or "Here is a new book that just came in the mail. It's sort of like the one we read last week, about the very hungry caterpillar. Let's take a look at it." These and other simple strategies build children's confidence that their secure foundation of past experiences will serve them well as they explore new activities and materials.

SECURITY THROUGHOUT THE YEAR: CRITICAL TIMES AND CHANGING NEEDS

Children's emotional security needs may change at different points in the year in response to transitions and developmental challenges. The emotion-centered teacher is aware of these ups and downs and ensures that children's needs are appropriately met.

Entering a New Program

A critical point in children's emotional security is, of course, the beginning of the year, or whenever the child enters the early childhood program. At any age (including adulthood), entry into a new setting brings uncertainty, anxiety, and a search for familiarity and stability. Depending on children's ages and previous experiences, they may cope with this transition through tears, tantrums, withdrawn or "babyish" behavior, quiet observation, frantic activity, and other strategies of varying effectiveness.

Experienced teachers have many ways to help children feel secure in their new setting (Griffin, 1997; Hendrick, 2000). Some visit the child at home; others ask each child to bring a family picture to school. When possible, many teachers have each child visit the program when other children are not present, to explore materials and check out the environment. Most high-quality programs encourage family members—the child's first secure base—to stay with their child for a time. Early in the year, teachers try to be prompt and explicit in orienting children to the new setting and meeting children's basic needs. "Here is a tissue for you, Robert," Natalie says warmly. "Now your nose will feel better." "Let's look at our chart to see what we will be doing right after lunch," says primary-grade teacher Hope, helping new children visualize the predictable sequence of the day.

In the first weeks, new children feel more secure with familiar activities that guarantee success. For example, kindergarten teacher Christine usually puts out play dough and simple construction materials early in the year, and she sets up the dramatic play area with basic household props. Books are selected to represent themes of family and home, with pictures reflecting the children's cultures and household compositions.

Emotion-centered teachers plan beginning-of-the-year activities to allow insecure children to watch from a distance or to participate in a low-key way. Edward preferred to sit in his cubby during music time for the first month of kindergarten, watching intently but never participating—until the day when his teacher got stuck on a verse of "Over in the Meadow" and Edward confidently filled in the missing words. In another class, 3-year-old Megan refused to participate in any indoor activities for the first few weeks, sitting forlornly near the door despite the staff's efforts. Only when she was outside on her favorite red tricycle (which, incidentally, was just like her trike at home) did she appear secure. The teacher moved some indoor equipment outside, and Megan triked over to the easel, where she painted picture after picture perched safely on her three-wheeled secure base.

Most children are more confident in a new setting if they are encouraged to bring special objects from home. For very young children, security blankets or beloved stuffed animals build emotional bridges between home and the child care setting. New children often will clutch the familiar object all day, but as time goes on they may need it only when they are sleepy or distressed. Rather than making children more insecure and dependent, these treasured objects often support exploration and learning in a new environment (Gay & Hyson, 1976; Steier & Lehman, 2000).

Older children rely less on concrete representations of security. However, they gain pride and confidence from sharing pictures and objects from home, especially at the beginning of the year. Some teachers have a special display table for children's prized objects; others create a bulletin board collage of photographs. One teacher creates a class book every fall, with a page for each child; another has each of her kindergartners create "a book about me and my family," with drawings and dictated descriptions of family, favorite foods and activities, and so on. The laminated books become part of the class library and can be borrowed overnight.

Finally, emotion-centered teachers provide beginning-of-the-year security by establishing and maintaining clear limits for children's behavior. Just as children feel better in a new situation when they know where the bathroom is and what happens after juice time, they also need to know what behavior is expected and what is not allowed. They need to know that teachers will protect them and other children from their own actions and will help them to figure out how to deal with arguments and fights. Despite the security that these limits provide, young children also need to be sure that teachers will not reject or abandon them if they violate classroom rules.

Losing a Special Caregiver

Typically, children's emotional security develops strong roots after the first weeks in a new program. However, children's security may be shaken when teachers leave during the year. With about one-third of all child care staff leaving their jobs each year, personnel changes have become a common occurrence in many child care centers. Children develop close relationships with early childhood teachers, relationships that can be very similar to the kinds of attachments that children develop with their parents (Howes & Ritchie, 2002). Infants and toddlers in full-time child care often develop an especially close attachment to one caregiver. If that caregiver leaves, sadness and distress may result.

Does this mean that such close attachments should be discouraged? Not at all. Close, loving relationships with parents and teachers allow children to explore, learn, and develop social and academic competence (Honig, 2002; Howes & Ritchie, 2002; Pianta, 1999). Nevertheless, the loss of a special caregiver is distressing and temporarily disruptive for a child. If the departure can be anticipated, it is important to talk with the child about the separation. Many people are reluctant to do this, knowing that children will be upset. Some teachers may think it's better to just disappear. This is never a good idea, as it undermines children's confidence that adults are trustworthy people. Instead, children can talk about the change, channel their feelings into creating mementos or planning a party for the teacher who is leaving, and begin to develop new relationships. Overlap between caregivers is advisable (but, unfortunately, not always practical in the context of teacher shortages) to provide continuity and to allow children to begin to see the new caregiver as a dependable source of support and comfort.

Working on Difficult Skills

As the year goes on, challenging new activities may shake children's emotional security. Children often experience a period of emotional disorganization when working on a new developmental achievement, even if the child chose the task herself (Brazelton, 1992). This disequilibrium requires a large dose of adult support. Even emotionally secure children may worry about failure or (especially if they are a bit older) looking "dumb" in their friends' eyes. But children do not need to be protected from every possible failure. A certain amount of challenge and even frustration helps children feel secure about their own ability to cope with difficulties. In a program that emphasizes child choice and cooperative learning, children feel more secure in trying new things. Like Hope's primary graders, children can help one another, learning that some people are great at cutting out Jell-O shapes while others are good at printing, spreading jam evenly, or counting play money.

Emotion-centered teachers are also aware that children's intensity when working on new skills often leads to frustration, exhaustion, and stress for children and adults alike. Teachers need to respect the child's drive toward mastery while also ensuring a healthy balance between intense bursts of work on new skills and relaxed times to settle into old, familiar activities.

CONCLUSION

Hope and other skilled teachers begin the job of building an emotion-centered program by establishing a foundation of emotional security. This chapter has shown how important this task is, whether the goal is to build on children's early, positive experiences or to compensate for insecure or even abusive family relationships. Although the physical environment and program organization contribute to emotional security, the teacher is the most crucial component of the secure environment.

It is not easy to be a child in an early childhood program. Imagine experiencing it for the first time. You come into a strange building full of other children and adults who are strangers, full of enticing toys that are not your own. Mysterious rituals are to be followed, for washing hands, for lining up, for waiting for turns at circle time. There are many things to learn about—but in order to learn you have to wade in and try things. Learning is hard work, and it involves taking risks. You have to pick up the guinea pig in order to find out what he looks like underneath. You have to make marks on the paper in order to print your name. You have to walk over to the blocks and start building in order to get some classmates to play with you. You have to pick up the red and green cubes if you want to try to make a pattern. All along the way, there are risks—risks of being laughed at, of being wrong, of being ignored or rejected. Yet this desire for mastery is what leads to social and intellectual competence. It is almost impossible for children to have the courage to start on this journey without a foundation of emotional security.

In Chapter 3 we will examine another strategy for implementing an emotion-centered curriculum. Terry, a family child care provider, will show us how a skilled practitioner can help children understand their own and others' feelings.

Helping Children Understand Emotions

"Oh, Mister Impatient!" Terry says with an affectionate laugh to baby Warren, who is wriggling and fussing in his infant seat on the floor. "Your breakfast is coming right up. Take a chill pill, sweetie." The toddlers in Terry's family child care home are finishing their toast and banana slices. Three of the children are triplets. One of them, Barry, has had continuing respiratory problems related to the triplets' premature birth and must have breathing treatments twice a day. "I know, Barry," says Terry calmly when Barry twists away from the mask. "It'll just take a couple of minutes and then we'll be all done for now." The other children look on from their high chairs as Barry breathes in the mist.

Music comes from the sunny family room, where Terry's sister-in-law, who helps with the children, has turned on the tape player. Doreen and Nina, the "big girls" at ages 3 and 4, are dancing on the carpet, twirling and grinning at each other. "Are you ready?" Terry asks the younger children as several of them protest and reach out to her from their seats in the kitchen. "Want to sing and dance now? Get down?" She sets each toddler on the floor with a hug and a friendly smile, and carries the youngest into the family room.

Doreen solemnly shows Terry a "booboo" on her knee, the scab barely visible. She tells Terry how she was riding her bike at her grandma's and "I fell off my bike. It was bleeding and I cried and cried." Several other children join in showing their scrapes and bruises as Terry listens and inspects the damage. Kisses and several colorful Band-Aids are applied.

Brenda, another of the triplets, has been having a hard time getting involved this morning. Sadly she wanders from group to group. "Brenda, what is it?" asks Terry. "Do you want your 'woober' [Brenda's name for her blanket]?" Brenda nods. "How's that, Brenda?" asks Terry, giving Brenda her blanket and settling her into the big armchair. "Maybe you got up too early. Let's see if you feel better in a little bit." Thumb in her mouth, Brenda contentedly watches the others from the chair.

Rachel has been walking for just 2 weeks. She staggers around the room, intent on her new independence. She moves toward a long chain of large beads that hangs from the ceiling. Three-year-old Doreen has been playing with the beads, sliding them up and down. Rachel squeals and grabs at the chain, yanking it away from Doreen and starting to cry as Doreen holds on grimly. Terry gently detaches Rachel's fingers from the chain. "Rachel says, 'I wanted that,'" Terry explains to Doreen as she hands Rachel another toy. "Maybe you can let her play with it in a few minutes."

In her family child care home, Terry provides many ingredients of a high-quality early childhood environment. Indoors and outdoors, the environment is child oriented, colorful, and inviting. Riding toys, puzzles, dramatic play props, a rabbit and guinea pigs, bird feeders, soft cushions, a playhouse in the yard—every feature of Terry's home reflects her understanding of young children's interests and needs. Each child, from 5-month-old Warren to 4-year-old Nina, is treated with personal, respectful, delighted attention. Ethnic and cultural diversity is welcomed, with Mexican American, African American, and white families represented among those served in Terry's rural program. As the number of Latino families in her community has increased, Terry has made a special effort to improve her Spanish language skills. Terry's husband, teenage children, and sister-in-law provide a warm extended family for the children in her care. Within this setting, Terry places an especially high priority on fostering children's understanding of their own feelings and the feelings of others.

Terry's priorities are consistent with much developmental research. Typically, children do become better at understanding emotions as they get older. Babies can distinguish angry faces from smiling ones, and toddlers can look at pictures of emotions and connect them with simple words that describe those feelings. By age 3, many children understand that feelings have causes—as long as the feelings and causes are simple. (Exploration 2 in Part II uses a vignette from another family child care home to illustrate these developmental trajectories in more detail, and it recommends readings to deepen understanding.) However, these changes in children's understanding do not happen automatically. And at any age, some children are more emotionally attuned than others.

Understanding emotions has many benefits. As pointed out earlier, preschoolers who understand how others may be feeling have better academic and social outcomes in later years (Izard et al., 2001). Children with greater knowledge of emotions are also more likely to behave sympathetically, to help those in distress and to share resources with others; in general, they are more socially competent (Denham, 1998; Saarni, 1999). Indeed, as children get older, failure to understand their own feelings and those of others is an indication of serious developmental problems. Abused children, for example, have a very hard time identifying emotions accurately (Camras, Sachs-Alter, & Ribordy, 1996). Children with autism can certainly feel and express emotion, but they have limited ability to understand why other people feel the way they do (Kasari & Sigman, 1996). Competence in emotional understanding contributes to children's overall positive development.

This chapter will begin by describing the elements of emotional understanding and will then show that developmental, individual, and sociocultural challenges may stand in the way of children's achievement of this understanding. Next I will demonstrate how early childhood professionals set the stage for understanding emotions by emphasizing conceptual development and by creating emotionally rich adult-child and peer interactions. Then we will look more closely at some specific strategies to encourage children's insights into their own and others' feelings. The chapter will end with cautions about excessive, intrusive, and inappropriate labeling of children's emotions.

THE "BASICS" OF EMOTIONAL UNDERSTANDING

What do children need to understand about emotions? The concepts that toddler Brenda, as well as the rest of Terry's children and other young children, are developing probably include the following "basics" (Saarni, 1990):

1. *Everyone has emotions.* I feel happy this morning. So does Brandon, and so does Barry. Terry, my caregiver, has feelings too. She is excited and surprised sometimes, and sometimes she is serious or unhappy.
2. *Emotions arise because of different situations.* Lots of things make me happy: my toast on my high chair tray, a hug from Terry, the click of beads on the chain when I tug it. When someone takes my toy, or when I fall off my bike, or when I just get tired after lunch, I get angry or sad.
3. *There are different ways of showing feelings.* Warren fusses a lot when he doesn't have something he really wants, like his bottle. Doreen just comes right over and grabs things. Nina tries to talk me into giving her my toys or gives something in trade. And sometimes I whine and pout.
4. *Other people may not feel the same way I do about everything.* When I am tired, I want my "woober," but Barry just sucks his thumb when he's tired. I like to ride around the patio on my trike very, very slowly, but Nina wants to go fast and get ahead of me.
5. *I can do things to change how I feel and how others feel.* When I'm sad, I can go sit in Terry's lap or in the big chair and after a while I feel better. Sometimes when baby Warren is fussing, I make funny faces at him, and he starts to laugh.

OBSTACLES TO UNDERSTANDING ABOUT FEELINGS

Children do not arrive at this emotional understanding quickly or automatically. As Exploration 3 in Part II emphasizes, developmental limitations, family and community environments, and cultural differences may create challenges along the way. Infants and very young children have only limited ability to infer the reasons for others' happiness, sadness, or anger. And even somewhat older children have a hard time drawing conclusions about the causes of emotion when the situation is unfamiliar, or when the other person's feelings are different from those the child would have. Young children may also have trouble understanding the cause-effect connections between an event and an emotional response, and they have particular difficulty understanding complex emotional experiences or mixed emotions (Denham, 1998).

Differences in family expressiveness (Dunsmore & Halberstadt, 1997; Halberstadt, Crisp, & Eaton, 1999) also influence children's ability to understand various emotional situations. Generally, more expressive families provide richer opportunities to develop emotional understanding. However, there are limits to the benefits of expressiveness. Conflict-ridden families and violent communities offer many emotionally intense experiences, but these environments often leave young children frightened, confused, and unable to process emotion signals in accurate, adaptive ways (Camras et al., 1996; Repetti, Taylor, & Seeman, 2002).

Finally, cultural contexts may complicate children's development of emotional understanding. For example, rules about how and when to show feelings may be easy for children to understand in the familiar culture of home and community. In Nina's Mexican American household, children are encouraged to express their feelings less intensely than is permitted in her family child care home. In a culturally diverse child care or school setting, the rules may be confusingly different. And for children whose home language differs from that of their early childhood program, even the words that represent feelings can be obstacles.

Teachers should not be discouraged by these multiple challenges to emotional understanding. Teachers can do more than just sit back and wait for children to mature. The emotion-centered professional will develop a rich array of strategies to help children of every age, family history, and cultural environment gain a better understanding of their own and others' feelings.

SETTING THE STAGE

Much positive learning about emotions occurs without direct adult instruction. Terry supports children's emotional understanding by establishing an environment that enhances concept development, by allowing children opportunities to experience, observe, and express feelings during spontaneous peer play, and by being attuned to teachable moments throughout the day.

Supporting General Concept Development

In many ways, learning about emotions parallels and is a product of children's understanding of many other concepts, such as time, space, number, and causality (Scholnick, Nelson, Gelman, & Miller, 1999). By supporting concept development and learning in all domains, early childhood professionals will simultaneously enhance children's understanding of concepts of emotion (see Resource Note 3.1 and Exploration 2 in Part II).

As in Terry's family child care home, children gain conceptual understanding when their learning is embedded in many real-world exemplars of a particular concept. Young children may use these exemplars to con-

RESOURCE NOTE 3.1 How Do People Learn?
(About Emotions and Other Things)

Children develop concepts about emotions the way they learn about many other things. In another National Research Council report, *How People Learn* (Bransford, Brown, & Cocking, 2000), the authors identify a small number of basic pathways by which children and adults gain knowledge of a variety of phenomena. These pathways can support children's learning about emotions in much the same way that they support learning about number, time, or place.

In general, research shows that people (from young children to mature adults) learn best when their environments are characterized in the following ways:

Learner-Centered

Children learn best when teachers respect and build on what children bring to the table—culture, beliefs, prior knowledge—and then help children connect what they already know with what they don't yet know.

Knowledge-Centered

Children also need well-organized, accessible knowledge, presented by teachers in developmentally appropriate ways. This principle applies to knowledge about emotions just as it does to knowledge about mathematics.

Assessment-Centered

Learning will be more powerful if teachers continuously assess what children are thinking (in this case, about emotions), and how they are thinking. With this knowledge, teachers can devise effective strategies to help children develop higher levels of understanding.

learning about emotions, will be stronger within "connected
care center, school, community agencies—all working together

ticular concepts, including concepts about
, & O'Conner, 2001). A child's mental
ple, comes to include not just the vocabu-
d causes, frequently observed sad situations,
ors.
ren are able to observe peers and adults express-
ty of ways—and having those emotions responded

to in a variety of ways—the better children are able to construct emotion concepts. Cognitive development is also supported when children see others using thinking skills effectively, and when children get many opportunities to practice their emerging skills in a social context with concrete materials and personally relevant situations (Berk & Winsler, 1995; Bodrova & Leong, 1995; Bredekamp & Rosegrant, 1992). Programs like Terry's ensure that children have these opportunities.

Promoting Emotion-Rich Peer Interactions

Children cannot understand emotions unless they have had many opportunities to experience, observe, and express them. Terry sets the stage for learning about feelings by allowing the children to interact with one another in spontaneous, unhurried blocks of time. Children are not hustled from one preplanned activity to the next, nor does Terry's homelike playroom even contain formally designated learning centers. Rather, for much of the day children invent interesting things to do with the many appropriate materials available in the house and yard. Terry supports these activities but knows when to step back and let the children play and learn together.

Close friendships have developed among Terry's children. Spending all day together 5 days a week, this small group has become extremely cohesive. Children in family child care often develop an intimacy much like that seen in sibling relationships. These peer relationships are important for the development of emotional understanding. Children express more of both positive and negative emotions when they are with friends—friendship seems to open the door to displays of all sorts of feelings (Hartup, Laursen, Stewart, & Eastenson, 1988; Maguire & Dunn, 1997). And these kinds of emotion-laden interactions, although often wearing on caregivers, provide young children with essential raw materials for the development of concepts about emotions.

Terry's program also incorporates personalized, unhurried routines that contain colorful emotional exchanges among children. Meals, naps, and toileting bring out children's joy, anger, disgust, surprise, pride, and virtually every other emotion. Because Terry's children are at such different developmental points, the emotional style of their responses differs in interesting ways. Terry vividly described the other children's fascination with the triplets' toilet-training adventures. Nina clapped and cheered from the bathroom doorway as Barry pulled down his pants all by himself. Rachel, younger than the triplets, followed each one on their frequent bathroom trips, peering curiously into the toilet before and after its use. Children spontaneously imitate one another's facial and vocal expressions of emotion. Waiting for Terry to dish up their spaghetti lunch, one child playfully called out "Mommy!" and immediately every child in the kitchen mock-plaintively chorused "Mommy, mommy, mommy,

mommy!" as Terry laughed and distributed their plates. At breakfast every day, the group closely observes Barry's protests and eventual acceptance of his breathing treatments—as well as Terry's calm handling of the procedure.

Identifying Prime Times for Understanding Feelings

Terry is also alert for "prime times" when she can heighten children's emotional understanding. Her affectionate one-on-one interactions offer an especially rich context. Whether cuddling, talking intimately, or sharing focused interest in a toy, a bird at the feeder, or a scraped knee, at these moments children seem especially receptive to learning about emotions. Conflict situations offer equally promising avenues for the children to learn about feelings. With infants, toddlers, and preschool children who know one another almost like siblings, Terry's group has inevitable clashes over possessions, turn taking, and status. Terry knows that these situations can help her give children insight into the causes and consequences of emotional expression. Terry's awareness of the possibilities embedded in these and other day-to-day events allows her to build a sound foundation for the development of emotional understanding.

STRATEGIES TO ENCOURAGE EMOTIONAL UNDERSTANDING

But setting the stage is not enough. In her family child care home, Terry uses many active strategies to enhance her children's understanding of their own and others' feelings. Like many other emotion-centered teachers, she relies more on informal, on-the-fly techniques than on isolated, formal lessons about emotions.

Emphasizing Activities That Support Understanding

In a corner of Terry's playroom, a cozy area has soft carpeting, doll beds, blankets, baby dolls, and toy telephones. Doreen and Nina have lifted several dolls out of a doll bed and are huddled in the corner with their "babies." Doreen holds some Band-Aids that Terry had dispensed earlier, when the children were showing her their scrapes and cuts. Doreen and Nina solemnly examine their babies for "booboos." "She gots one right here," Doreen says, showing Nina a spot on her doll's leg. "*Dale un beso,*" Nina recommends, kissing the doll. "Oh, no!" exclaims Doreen dramatically. "My baby's hurt! She's hurt bad!" "*Dame el teléfono,*" says Nina, waving her arms at the phone. Dropping the babies, they race to get the play telephone. "Mommy, mommy, help! Help!" shrieks Doreen into the mouthpiece.

"Come help the baby!" Terry, smiling, moves closer. "Do you need a mommy to help?"

Pretend play is critically important for learning about emotions. Home observations of toddlers showed that pretend play situations were among the most frequent occasions for children to use emotion language and to act out emotionally vivid scenes (Dunn & Brown, 1991). As with Doreen and Nina's doll play, Terry promotes similar opportunities by providing materials, support, and well-timed collaboration. No soap opera can match the high drama of a typical scene of spontaneous pretend play. The feelings that are enacted and reenacted provide rich material for emotional understanding.

For this to happen, though, adults need to avoid the risks of over-involvement and overstructuring. Some early childhood programs channel all pretend play into preplanned themes that tie in with curriculum units and specific academic goals: "Today, boys and girls, the dramatic play area is set up as an art museum. You can pay admission, look at paintings, and give me a tour." These efforts often result in play that, while pleasing to adults and easy to manage, is emotionally flat, allowing few opportunities for children to express, experience, and construct a genuine understanding of the rich tapestry of human emotion. (It is heartening, however, to see how children will subvert adult-dominated play to their own ends, with "robbers" showing up to steal the art exhibit's paintings, or a frisky "dog" disrupting a dull pretend museum tour.) In contrast to teacher-planned pretend play, emotional understanding is especially enhanced by the kind of free-form personalized fantasies woven by Terry's children, who have been given time, space, and raw materials with which to pretend, and whose affective liveliness is respected and gently guided by responsive adults.

In addition to pretend play, many other activities and materials will support the development of emotional understanding. Well-chosen books, songs, and videotapes can help children understand their own and others' feelings. Creative arts activities allow children to portray emotions in a variety of media and to compare their portrayals with those of other children. For older children, writing offers yet another tool to explore the meaning of emotion-related experiences. Later chapters show how teachers can use these same activities to help children express and regulate their feelings.

This chapter de-emphasizes the use of formal activities and lessons to help children understand emotions. For the early childhood professional seeking suggestions, numerous resources are available. Books and games about feelings—either those "about" certain feelings or those portraying relevant, emotionally rich situations—can be valuable additions to the early childhood program. Examples are listed in Resource Note 3.2. The programs for social and emotional learning described in Appendix B can be useful addition to more informal activities.

However, there is a risk in becoming overly dependent on specialized activities or programs to build children's understanding of emotions.

RESOURCE NOTE 3.2 Books and Activities to Promote
Young Children's Understanding Of Emotions

Books

A few of the many books that lend themselves to rich discussions of emotions are listed here.

Glad Monster, Sad Monster: A Book About Feelings (1997). Anne Miranda and Ed Emberley. New York: Little, Brown.
On Monday When It Rained (1989). Cherryl Kachenmeister . Boston: Houghton Mifflin.
How Are You Peeling? Foods with Moods (1999). Saxton Freymann and Joost Elffers. New York: Arthur A. Levine Books.
Feelings (1986). Aliki. New York: Greenwillow.
When Sophie Gets Angry—Really, Really Angry. . . . (1999). Molly Garrett Bang. New York: Scholastic.
Quiet As a Mouse!: A Moving Picture Storybook (2002). Richard Powell. Wilton, Conn.: Tiger Tales.
Big Book of Beautiful Babies (2001). David Ellwand. New York: Dutton.
The Feel Good Book (2002). Todd Parr. Boston: Little, Brown.
My Many Colored Days (1998). Dr. Seuss. New York: Knopf.

Simple Games and Other Activities

Here are a few examples of how you might use everyday games to support children's understanding of emotions and to develop emotion language.

Feeling Dice. Make cubes out of small gift boxes or milk cartons. Put a different feeling face on each side. Fill with beans for added fun! Children roll the dice. They identify the feeling it lands on and tell about a time they felt that way.

Feeling Wheel. Replace the colors on a Twister game or make your own spinning wheel that features feeling faces on each space. Leave one space a blank face. Children spin the wheel. They identify the feeling on the wheel and tell about a time they felt that way. If the spinner lands on the blank face, they say how they are feeling at that moment.

Pass the Hat. Fill a hat or large envelope with pictures from magazines and children's catalogs of different feeling faces. Play some music. As the music plays, the children pass the hat. When the music stops, the child picks out a face and identifies it. They can describe a time when they felt that way, and then pass the hat again when the music starts.

Mirror Magic. Provide each child or pair of children with a hand-held mirror. Play the song "Feelings" by Hap Palmer. Each time the song requests that children "show me how you feel when you're feeling angry [happy, sad, and so on]," the children make the face in the mirror and then show their partner.

On Monday When. This activity emphasizes the point that feelings can change. Children paint or draw a picture about how they are feeling on Monday and why (teachers can write the reason for them). Then on Friday, children do the same activity. The teacher can put together a class book that emphasizes how everyone was feeling on Monday and how their feelings may have changed 5 days later.

Feeling Charades. Prepare an envelope with different feeling faces. Children, one at a time, get to pick a feeling face, without saying what it is. The child makes the face and body language, even tone of voice to go with the feeling, and the other children guess the feeling.

(continued)

RESOURCE NOTE 3.2 *(continued)*

If You're Happy and You Know It. You can play this game using a variety of different emotions—"If you're happy and you know it, clap your hands . . . if you're scared and you know it, hide your eyes . . . if you're angry and you know it, stomp your feet"—and invite children to make up new verses for this favorite song.

Note: Adapted from Joseph & Strain (in press). For additional recommendations, see the Web site of the Center for the Social and Emotional Foundations of Early Learning (*http://csefel.uiuc.edu*).

Children construct concepts out of many interrelated experiences, not in a one-shot lesson (Bransford, Brown, & Cocking, 2000). Having closets full of emotion-related books and activities at their disposal, some teachers may neglect the developmentally more important learning that can be embedded in spontaneous play, daily interactions, and routines. They may also send children contradictory messages about emotions, as when teachers use isolated, scripted lessons about feelings but are harsh, cold, or insensitive when the lesson is over. With these cautions in mind, though, teacher-planned activities and resources, or well-evaluated programs on social and emotional learning, can be a useful part of a more comprehensive approach to support children's emotional understanding.

Mirroring Children's Emotion Expressions

> Terry sits on a low armchair holding baby Warren. He gazes intently into her face and begins to smile. Looking down, Terry smiles back, raising her brows in spontaneous imitation of Warren's facial expression and tipping her head back and forth. Warren squeals in pleasure and smiles even more broadly.

Emotions develop within a social context. Expressions like Warren's smile are indeed universal and innate, but Warren's understanding of his own and others' feelings depends on having those emotions reflected, imitated, and amplified. Most parents intuitively copy many of their infants' emotion expressions, shifting from interest to joy to surprise to distress as their babies' faces display each of these feelings (Malatesta-Magai, 1991). Family child care providers and other professionals behave in much the same way—fortunately, because these face-to-face "imitation games" have clear developmental benefits, exposing children to many thousands of examples of emotion expressions that reflect and implicitly comment on children's own feelings. At the same time, Warren and other babies are beginning to learn that their emotions can influence other people (Dunn, Brown, & Beardsall, 1991) and can communicate a "feeling state" that others share too.

Responding to Children's Feelings

> Brenda has been kneeling on the patio looking into the guinea pigs' cage, an expression of interest and longing on her face. Terry comes over and unlatches the cage. She lifts one of the guinea pigs out and places it on Brenda's lap. Brenda shrinks back a little as the guinea pig wiggles around. Terry smiles reassuringly and keeps one hand on Brenda's leg while touching the guinea pig with her other hand. "Oooh," says Brenda, giggling nervously. "Silky's scratching me." "Here," responds Terry, "let's give Silky some nice touches." Terry strokes the guinea pig gently as Brenda watches. Tentatively, Brenda extends her hand and pats Silky on the back. As Terry and Brenda look at Silky, Doreen walks by them several times, alone amidst the children riding trikes on the patio. Terry looks up. "Are you lost, little girl?" she asks warmly. "Come sit by us for a while."

Emotions can communicate in powerful ways. Terry is sensitively attuned to her children's emotional states. Out on the patio, she noticed Brenda's interest in the guinea pigs and followed up on it by taking Silky out of his cage. When Brenda shrank back and appeared fearful, Terry acted calmly and reassuringly. And Terry responded to Doreen's nonverbal expressions of sadness and aimlessness, inviting Doreen to join her and Brenda. Responses like Terry's—"contingent" on what children do—are valuable both to the children who are directly involved and to other children who observe Terry's words and actions.

These kinds of interactions help children realize that their emotions can have consequences. Children find out that other people understand something about their inner states if they show their feelings in verbal or nonverbal ways. If they are fortunate enough to have a sensitive parent or caregiver like Terry, children also learn that they can rely on adult responses to help them feel better when they are sad, to share their joy when they are happy, or to place supportive limits around them when they lose control.

Labeling Children's Emotions

> Warren has been sitting in his bouncing seat for some time now, watching the older children drawing with chalk on the cement patio. He begins to whimper and then to wail, twisting his body as if to get out of the seat. "Well, well," says Terry to Warren. "Are you mad? Do you want to draw too, buddy?"

She lifts him out of the seat and hugs him. "Are you happy now that you got up here?"

Young children have a wide range of feelings but do not come equipped with language to talk about these feelings. Terry often provides emotion labels to describe what the children in her group may be feeling. The terms *mad, happy,* and *sad* are frequently heard in Terry's family child care home, along with other emotion language like *wants to, likes it,* and *what's the matter?* Besides validating children's emotion expressions, Terry's simple words and phrases—with their Spanish equivalents—begin to give all the children categories of emotions that help their understanding.

These emotion labels also introduce children to the ways that their own culture, or that of the adult, categorizes emotional states. Terry's labels of *happy* and *mad* are typical of Western definitions, but other cultures may vary. For example, some African languages use the same label for anger and sorrow; one Alaskan Inuit group has separate labels for fear of physical harm (*iqhi*) and fear of being treated unkindly (*ilira*) (Russell, 1989).

Talking About Causes of Feelings

Terry's children are in the playroom cleaning up before lunch. Rachel stoops down and stands up again quickly, whining and pouting. "Rachel, what is it?" Terry asks with concern. "Did you hit your head under the table?" As the children finish cleaning up, Terry wipes their faces, saying to several protesters, "I know, I know; no one likes to have their faces washed." As Terry walks past him, Warren again begins to fuss, holding out his arms. "Did you think I was going to pick you up, Warren?" Terry asks. "I will in just a minute." Nina tries to help Abel button his pants, but 4-year-old Abel pushes her hands away angrily, as Nina looks pleadingly at Terry. "Nina, *el no quiere que tú hagas eso*—he doesn't want you to do that," explains Terry. "He wants to do it himself today."

With these and other comments, Terry frequently and informally talks with her children about why they feel the way they do. As we have seen, emotion-related conversations help young children understand their own emotions and those of others. These kinds of conversations go beyond simply providing labels for feelings; rather, Terry and other emotion-focused early childhood professionals talk about the causes of these feelings. Through many such experiences, children begin to understand that different emotions may have different causes, and that different people may feel angry or happy for different reasons. Such conversations, embedded in daily routines, highlight these concepts and help children better understand others' perspectives (Dunn et al., 1991).

OVERLABELING: SOME CAUTIONS

In encouraging early childhood professionals to mirror, label, and interpret feelings for children, we need to emphasize that this approach can be—and often is—carried to extremes. There is a big difference between Terry's informal, lighthearted approach and a heavy-handed overinvolvement in children's every emotional nuance.

Guidelines for developmentally appropriate practices (Bredekamp & Copple, 1997) can help teachers decide when and how to use the strategies outlined above. At different ages, children may benefit from different approaches to emotional understanding. Mirroring or copying children's nonverbal emotion expressions is especially appropriate and important in face-to-face exchanges with infants. Providing emotion labels is probably most important when children are just developing language skills. And interpreting the underlying reasons for others' emotional reactions becomes increasingly important as children develop friendships and broader social interests, from age 2 onward. But as children move toward the school-age years, they often resent adults telling them what they are feeling inside. Just as they are developing a greater desire for privacy in their personal habits and friendships, they may seek emotional privacy as well. Sensitive adults allow children this privacy while remaining attuned to their needs.

Developmental appropriateness goes beyond these age-related considerations. Children's individual and cultural characteristics must also be taken into account. Children whose family life has provided few opportunities to learn about emotions may need more frequent, more explicit labeling and interpretation of feelings and more focused, formal interventions to increase emotional understanding (Denham, 1998; Raver, 2002). Early childhood programs that include children with disabilities find that extra effort is needed to help everyone understand the varied ways that people can express emotions. And in every case, culture creates a context for decisions about which interventions may best support emotional understanding.

CONCLUSION

In this chapter we have seen that early childhood professionals have countless ways to develop emotional understanding in children. By laying a foundation of emotionally vivid interactions, and by mirroring, responding to, labeling, and conversing about feelings, Terry and other skilled practitioners enhance children's ability to understand their own emotional responses and those of others. In turn, this ability fosters children's social competence, empathy, and perspective-taking ability. Resource Note 3.3 summarize these strategies for day-to-day use.

RESOURCE NOTE 3.3 Strategies to Help Young Children Understand Emotions

1. Provide daily activities that prompt children to think about emotions.
   • Promote/pretend play
   • Share/emotion-rich books
   • Weave/creative arts throughout the curriculum.

2. Smile, look interested, look sad: Show your own feelings and mirror children's own expressions of emotions.
   • Engage babies in "imitation games."
   • Let children see that their own expressions influence others' reactions.

3. Respond to what children are feeling.
   • Tune in to children's faces, bodies, and voices.
   • Use this information to construct prompt, sensitive appropriate responses.

4. Name children's feelings.
   • Give words to what children experience emotionally.
   • Connect the emotion labels that you use with children's cultures.

5. Talk about the causes of feelings.
   • Help children connect the way they feel with what made them feel that way.
   • Use these conversations to build children's ability to see others' points of view.

But understanding emotions is not enough. Early childhood professionals also want children to behave in ways that are emotionally genuine, direct, and appropriate within a particular setting and cultural context. In Chapter 4, we will see how kindergarten teacher Christine's active use of modeling becomes a powerful strategy for emotional socialization.

Modeling Genuine, Appropriate Emotional Responses

The kindergarten children were sitting in a circle on the rug. Christine, their teacher, had just finished explaining that they would be doing the "weekend news" a different way today (every Monday morning the class has been dictating news of their weekend doings, as a language and literacy activity). Today, Christine explained, the children would pair up and tell their weekend news to each other. After they finished, they would return to the circle, where each person would then tell the partner's news to the rest of the group. Christine finished her explanation and paused for effect. "Kids, look at me. *This is hard*," she said emphatically, with a serious tone of voice and a sad facial expression. "You might forget your partner's news, or you might leave something out. That's okay, because you've never done this before." Her tone and facial expression began to brighten at this point, and she looked intently at each child in the group. "But we'll be doing this today, and next week, and the week after that. And you know what?" Christine asked, still brighter and more confident sounding, and continuing to

65

look at each child in the group. "You'll get better and better at remembering, because you'll be getting so much practice!" She ended with a firm nod and a wide grin.

Practitioners who adopt an emotion-centered curriculum have clear developmental goals. Among other things, the emotion-centered teacher wants children to associate positive emotions with problem solving and effortful intellectual activities, to begin to control their emotional expressions when they might be hurtful to others, and to use language to talk about their own and others' emotions. This chapter will focus on an especially powerful strategy—the teacher's *modeling* of genuine, appropriate emotional responses.

Children learn from observing other people, getting ideas of how new kinds of behavior are performed, and using these ideas to guide their actions (Bandura, 1977). Modeling and other kinds of observations are seen as especially important by writers who are influenced by "social learning theory" (see Exploration 1 in Part II). Parents and teachers know that young children can remember and copy even complex behaviors that they see. This modeling (Bandura 1977, 1986; Schunk & Zimmerman, 1997) can occur even when the model—the person being observed—is not aware of being watched, and when the child is not directly rewarded for noticing and remembering the model's behavior.

Parents are the child's first models and remain the most significant influences for the majority of children. However, early childhood teachers are also important models. Children may spend as much as 10 hours a day in their teachers' company. As children get older, they increasingly look for models beyond the family. Teachers, coaches, club leaders, adult friends, TV characters—all may be observed and imitated. The child's repertoire of behavior, personality characteristics, and values becomes colored by the behavior, characteristics, and values modeled by a significant adult.

In this chapter, I will describe how adults model emotions for children and how these encounters influence children's emotional development. Then we will see how these processes are actually used in early childhood programs. I will suggest effective strategies that practitioners can use to increase the likelihood that children will imitate desired patterns of emotion expression. The chapter will close with a consideration of some complexities and difficulties in adults' decisions about emotion modeling.

MODELING EMOTIONS

Adults As Emotion Models

In the example at the beginning of this chapter, Christine was doing much more than simply describing a new variation on an activity. As Christine previewed the activity, her face, voice, and language presented children with a mixture of emotions. Christine showed that she thought of the "partner news" as a serious, difficult task, that difficult tasks require effort, and that they may initially cause some frustration. When she said that children might forget their partners' information, her tone and language acknowledged the possibility of disappointment and failure. But she also described with interest and joy the gradual improvement she expected to see and showed that she was allied with the children in working toward that long-term goal.

Christine was serving as an "emotion model" for her kindergarten children. Teachers, parents, and others provide children with models of how to express emotions, when to express emotions, how emotions are managed or regulated, how emotions are labeled, and how emotions can be interpreted and understood (Denham, 1998; Eisenberg et al., 2001). The resources in Exploration 3 in Part II offer additional help in investigating this and other important factors.

Fortunately, children are innately interested in adults' expressions of emotion, watching their faces and listening carefully to their tone of voice. Starting as early as 12 months, children are especially likely to look to adults for emotional information in new, uncertain situations, a process that has been called "social referencing" (Klinnert, Campos, Sorce, Emde, & Svejda, 1983; Walden & Ogan, 1988).

Effects of Adults' Emotion Modeling

Even babies imitate adults' expressions of emotion. When facial expressions of mothers and infants are videotaped and coded, it is easy to see how mothers' emotions influence their babies. It almost seems as if the babies watch for changes in their mothers' expressions and are primed to respond with their own expression changes. Among the participants in one such study (Malatesta & Haviland, 1982), certain mother-infant pairs had very similar expressive styles. A mother who frequently raised her eyebrows was likely to have a baby who did the same thing, and a mother who smiled a great deal often had a smiley child. And over several months, babies' expressive styles tended to become even more like their mothers'.

Adults' modeling of emotion expressions also sends children messages about new and possibly risky situations. For example, when a stranger approaches, babies typically turn and look at mother or other primary caregiver—if mother smiles and looks friendly, the baby is much more likely to behave in a friendly way herself. Similarly, when a crawling baby gets near an area that might be hazardous, it's typical (but not universal) for the baby to search the mother's face or even listen to her voice, apparently looking for information about her emotional response (Blackford & Walden, 1998; Klinnert et al., 1983). Infant and toddler teachers find that babies do the same in child care.

As children get older, their observation of adults continues to give them important information about emotions and about how to cope with emotion-laden situations. For example, children who often see adults showing empathy, generosity, and frustration tolerance are more likely to develop these qualities themselves (Eisenberg & Fabes, 1998). And adults' modeling of angry or constructive responses to conflict can have lasting impact on young children (See Resource Note 4.1).

EMOTION MODELING IN EARLY CHILDHOOD PROGRAMS

Early childhood educators should not be content to leave the important emotion modeling process entirely to chance. Competent, thoughtful professionals consciously decide what emotions and emotion-related behavior to model. They identify opportunities for emotion modeling in the daily program, and they take steps to increase the effectiveness of modeling on children's development and behavior.

Selecting Emotion-Related Targets for Modeling

Deciding which specific emotions or emotion-related behaviors to model is a question of values and personal philosophy. It also depends on the developmental level of the children in a particular class and on the

---

RESOURCE NOTE 4.1 Adults as Models: The Act Against Violence Project

Beginning in 1997, NAEYC, the American Psychological Association, and the Ad Council, Inc., have been involved in the ACT Against Violence project—Adults and Children Against Violence.

The project aims to send the message that early childhood is a time when children readily learn about violence from the adults around them. Watching and listening to adults, young children may learn that aggressive and violent responses to conflict and stress are okay, or they may learn that there are better, peaceful ways of dealing with difficult situations. How adults manage their own anger and how they approach emotion-laden situations make a big difference in children's own reactions. And children who learn effective ways of dealing with these situations are less likely to engage in violent behavior in later years.

Using a media campaign of television, radio, and print ads; a Website of resources including materials for families and teachers; and a community training component, ACT works to develop understanding of and commitment to these important roles for adults, whether they are parents, other family members, or early childhood professionals.

Learn more about ACT on-line (*www.actagainstviolence.org*).

teacher's knowledge of their earlier experiences, strengths, and needs. The examples below reflect Christine's priorities, her personality, and the characteristics of the children in her class, and the list is far from exhaustive.

Joy and Pleasure in Personal Relationships. Christine wants children to find pleasure in working and playing with others. She finds many opportunities to model this in her own relationships with children and adults in the classroom.

> Christine was seated at a table, engrossed in conversation with the father of one of the kindergarten children. A child who had been out of school for the past week came into the room. Immediately Christine interrupted her chat and exclaimed in a delighted tone, "*Here* she is! Hi, Patricia, I *missed* you!" which she accompanied by a hug and a pat on the back. "If you stay away this long, you get to do the calendar when you come back."

Interest and Curiosity. Interest—what some may call curiosity—seems to be a fundamental human emotion (Renninger, Hidi, & Krapp, 1992). Teachers can serve as important models of interest and fascination in finding out more about the world.

> As a way of assigning partners for "weekend news," Christine had given each child one half of a picture to match with another child's half. After the children found their partners by matching puzzle pieces, they were asked to come up in pairs and show the pictures to Christine. As each pair came up, Christine sincerely displayed curiosity about who got paired with whom and about their completed puzzle. "Who's your partner, Tim? Ricardo's your partner. Hi, Ricardo; you're Tim's partner for the news, huh? What did you and Ricardo get? Oh, a camel! Isn't that great?"

Anyone listening to this exchange repeated for each of 10 pairs of children would be impressed by the real curiosity and warmth behind Christine's comments. Her interest showed the children that working with new people and solving puzzles together were activities worthy of emotional involvement.

Tolerance for Frustration. As a kindergarten teacher, Christine knows her children are beginning to encounter learning tasks that they will find both challenging and frustrating. As Katz (1995) has emphasized, not all learning is fun, and not all learning is easy. Feelings of disappointment, annoyance, and even anger may interfere with the acquisition of important academic skills. Christine tries to help children cope with these feelings by letting them observe her own emotional responses to frustration and failure.

> Early one morning Christine was putting up a bulletin board. As she tried to staple a sheet of paper, the stapler kept jamming. Almost talking to herself, she muttered, "I am *so* annoyed with this stapler. It is *not* working right. I really want to get this bulletin board finished, and I can't if this stapler is broken." As Christine opened the stapler, she said, "Let me see, now. Ah-ha! There's a staple stuck in it. Let me see if I can poke it out. Yes! *Now* maybe I can get this bulletin board up."

To the few children who happened to be watching, this informal running commentary (done in Christine's typical, slightly exaggerated style, with much gesturing) showed that even grown-ups encounter frustrating situations. Christine also demonstrated that frustration could be expressed in words. And finally, Christine modeled a constructive response that was motivated by her feelings of frustration: She worked hard to fix the annoying stapler.

Pride in Hard Work. Christine deliberately points out to children that learning is hard at times. She emphasizes, however, that accomplishing difficult tasks makes you feel great, and that the harder the task, the greater the feelings of pride, joy, and satisfaction when the task is finally completed.

> Christine described to the class an art project they could do, in which they could make "stained glass windows" with colored tissue paper and starch. She seriously and carefully described the process that would have to be followed by the children who chose this activity. It involved a number of steps (selecting colors, cutting the tissue, placing it between sheets of black paper, letting the starch dry) spread out over several days. Christine then turned to the windows in the classroom, pointed to them, and said with great feeling, "Then, when the stained glass windows are all done, I'm going to climb up on a stepladder and hang every one of them right there. The sun will shine right through the colors in the tissue paper. Every one will be different, and they will look *so beautiful*."

Finding Opportunities for Emotion Modeling

Once the priorities for emotion modeling have been selected, teachers need to let children observe these emotions and behaviors. Emotion modeling should permeate all aspects of classroom life. Too often, though,

deliberate emotion modeling occurs only in response to children's misbehavior, or during formal periods devoted to "affective education," using a
packaged script and lesson plans unrelated to other aspects of the program.
In an emotion-centered program, teacher modeling of genuine, appropriate emotional expression is deliberately integrated into every kind of activity and every kind of adult-child interaction. Some modeling may take
place as the teacher goes about her own routine activities. It may also happen in one-to-one or small-group interactions with children, by simply
adding an emotion-modeling component to child- or teacher-initiated learning activities. Finally, teachers can deliberately model emotional responses
in activities planned or adapted for that purpose.

Teachers' Routine Activities. Like Christine with the recalcitrant stapler,
all early childhood teachers are constantly engaged in routine housekeeping tasks that call forth varied emotions and emotion-related behavior: finding materials, cleaning up spills, dealing with visitors, losing a form to be
sent to the principal's office, setting up a learning center. Teachers also share
their emotional responses to events in their out-of-school lives: their own
children's successes, vacation planning, car trouble. Children watch, remember, and learn from their teachers' emotional reactions in these day-
to-day contexts.

Joint Activity with Children. In a developmentally appropriate early childhood program, teachers are often involved in children's activities. As they
sit at a table or on the floor together, teacher and child may focus their attention on a set of blocks, a book, a puzzle, a lump of clay, or a tray of collage materials. Teachers can take advantage of these times of "shared focus"
or "joint attention" (Moore & Dunham, 1995; Trevarthen & Aitken, 2001)
to model a variety of desirable emotional responses. Working collabora-
tively or in parallel with the child, the teacher can let the child see her handle
the materials and link her activity to her feelings. With facial expressions,
words, and actions, teachers are able to demonstrate interested engagement
in challenging tasks, surprise at unexpected outcomes, and pleasure at success. Children are especially susceptible to this kind of modeling when they
are in new, uncertain situations. In deciding how to feel, they rely heavily
on their teacher's emotional response to the new challenge they are facing
together.

Responses to Children's Behavior. Children's spontaneous behavior provides an open door for emotion-related modeling. One example will illustrate the possibilities.

> Christine was on the playground. She saw a group of boys
> building with some large wooden crates. They had made a high,
> teetering structure, higher than was allowed by the rules of the

class. Christine walked over to the group. With widened eyes she commented on the high building they had made and said that it looked like they had worked really hard on it. Then her facial expression changed from surprise and pride to sadness. In a sincerely regretful tone of voice, Christine told them that the building had to be taken down. Looking carefully at each child, and with a slightly fearful expression, she explained, "This is *so* high. I'm worried that it could fall and hurt you guys."

In this example, Christine demonstrated how emotions might be connected with specific events or situations (pride at their skill in building; sadness when she had to request the structure's demolition; fear at the thought of injury to the children). Her facial expressions, voice, and language modeled concern and empathy at the same time that she matter-of-factly enforced a standing rule of the school. The impact of this emotion modeling was evident when one boy who was talking with Christine unconsciously echoed her facial expressions.

Teacher-Planned Opportunities. In addition to all of these informal settings for emotion modeling, teachers may create more formal, planned opportunities to model emotion-related behavior.

Christine, for example, often uses skits in her class. Sometimes the children produce their own skits, but she also uses skits acted by herself and her student teachers for a variety of purposes. Sometimes the skits introduce the children to a new activity or highlight a class problem that will be discussed at a later group time. One morning, she and her student teacher acted out the roles of a customer and a cleaning company employee, to demonstrate the procedures the children were to use when they later played "spring cleaning." Besides going over the rules for use of the equipment and showing how the children might write down orders and record payments, Christine and the student teacher modeled great interest in and enjoyment of the challenging tasks of taking orders and systematically cleaning the classroom.

Similarly, teachers have used puppets and dolls to demonstrate emotion-related behavior. Although the teacher is not actually the model in these kinds of activities, she controls the "script" and creates the conditions for modeling to take place. Especially when dealing with emotions that may be difficult for the teacher to express directly, or that may not occur frequently in the classroom, these tools are very helpful. For example, puppets may model the expression of emotions at the loss of a friend. Puppets may cry, express sadness and anxiety verbally, and comfort each other. Dolls could model ways of coping with fear after a violent incident or could be used to demonstrate empathic responses to others' distress.

It is easy to overlook some of these opportunities to model emotions. Resource Note 4.2 provides a few simple examples and reminders.

RESOURCE NOTE 4.2 Finding Opportunities to Model Emotions
for the Children You Teach

Check yourself: Are you finding the following opportunities to model emotions?

- Showing children how you feel as you prepare a tasty snack or try to fix a tricycle
- Getting involved in challenging, enjoyable "joint activities" in which you and your children can share feelings together
- Watching for times when you can react spontaneously—with interest, surprise, amazement—to what children are doing
- Planning occasional activities that demonstrate specific emotional reactions—a skit, a puppet show, doll dramas

---

Using the Characteristics of Effective Emotion Models

Christine is a very effective model. A visitor to her class is struck by how much children want to be like Christine, even in small behaviors. One sees children unconsciously copying Christine's mannerisms and some of her typically exuberant outbursts ("Get outta *town!*" is one of her favorites, often used in mock incredulity when a child tells her about some particularly exciting accomplishment). But beyond this superficial imitation, children are also reproducing Christine's attitudes toward work, her ways of using materials, and her ways of acting toward others.

Not all teachers are as successful as Christine in having children notice, remember, and reproduce their emotion-related modeling. Christine has developed many characteristics that are associated with effective modeling (Bandura, 1977,1986; Schunk & Zimmerman, 1997; see also Resource Note 4.3 and the discussion of social learning theories in Exploration 1 in Part II).

Nurturance. Children model themselves on nurturant adults like Christine.

> The children were taking attendance one morning. Sean had just come back from a 3–day absence. "Sean, what was wrong with you?" Christine asked in a concerned tone of voice, leaning forward from her low chair in the circle. "I missed you." "Sean wasn't sick!" one of the other children called out. "I know it, because he was at Amber's birthday party." "Well, you weren't here anyway, were you, Sean?" Christine continued.

RESOURCE NOTE 4.3 How to Increase the Odds That Children
Will Model Their Emotional Behavior on You

- Be *nurturing*
  Children will imitate adults who care for them and meet their physical and emotional needs.
- *Use your power to influence children in positive ways.*
  As a teacher and classroom leader, you have more power than you may think. Children model themselves on those who hold the key to the resources they desire—not candy and stickers, but your attention and sincere approval.
- *Show children how you are similar to them.*
  People tend to imitate those who resemble them in some way. While remaining the "grown-up," let children see the many ways in which you share their interests and feelings.

"You were out of school Wednesday, Thursday, and Friday. I really missed you."

There are many ways to be nurturant. Christine is not a quietly serene teacher who exudes calm acceptance and gentle warmth. Christine's style of nurturance is more exuberant and direct. She is affectionate with children, but her affection is expressed in a "buddy" pattern. Christine is a dominant physical presence in the room. She spontaneously finds opportunities to touch, nudge, drape an arm around, and share a laugh with the children in her kindergarten class. This nurturant quality "primes the pump" for children to attend to and respond to an adult model's behavior.

Power. Christine is powerful without being controlling or harsh. It is obvious to the children that she is in charge of the classroom, and that she holds the key to resources they desire and value.

Just before free-choice time, Christine was describing how the children could use various kinds of equipment to clean up the room (the class was exploring a project theme of "spring cleaning" that week). She gave them explicit guidelines for how to take things off the shelves, how to wash and dry the shelves, and how to replace the materials where they found them. "If I notice that things are getting messier and not cleaner, I'll have to say, 'Sorry, kids, you can't use the cleaning equipment.'"

Another time, Christine had been telling a small group of children about a new game in the math area. In a confident tone, she told the children, "This game is harder than the other ones—but you are such smart kindergarten children. I'm the teacher, and I'm supposed to keep making things harder for you, so you'll keep learning new things. That's my job."

Although Christine uses her power sparingly (having a classroom with many choices and few rules), the children are very aware of it. Christine is an important figure to the children, and as a result children pay attention to everything she says and does.

Similarity. People—including young children—are also likely to notice and imitate those whom they perceive to be similar to them in some way.

As Martina hung up her jacket, she told Christine that she had gone to the ballet over the weekend. "Oh, great!" Christine exclaimed with enormous delight and enthusiasm. "I wish I could have gone with you. I love the ballet." The other children snickered. "No, I really do," Christine insisted. "But it was *little* kids' ballet," Martina explained. "I love little kids' ballet too," Christine responded.

As the children took their places in the circle after exchanging weekend news with their partners, Bruce leaned over and said to Christine, "I think it's nice to sit next to your partner." "It *is* nice," answered Christine, rubbing Bruce's head. "I like it, too, Bruce."

Christine's personality and her interactions with the children serve to highlight similarities. She knows and shares many of the children's interests, and she makes a point of noting the things they have in common. Although children are more apt to model themselves on adults of the same gender, Christine is able to overcome this. She has a style of interaction that seems appealing both to girls and boys. She genuinely enjoys a bit of rough and tumble play on the playground, she likes sports, and she sometimes adopts a joking, almost teasing style of conversation that strikes an especially responsive chord with some of the kindergarten boys.

Enhancing Children's Imitation of Adult Emotion Models

Even if children perceive that an adult is nurturant, powerful, and similar to them, they may not model themselves on the adult. By attending to several other factors, early childhood professionals can raise the odds that children will imitate desired patterns of emotion.

Child Focus. In order for modeling to take place, children must focus on the model's behavior. Adults can increase the chances of imitation if they deliberately focus the child's attention on the behaviors to be modeled. Christine does this frequently and naturally. She will often preface a statement with, "Children, watch me" or "Listen to this," and then will wait until she has the children's attention. As in the example at the beginning of the chapter, her deliberate pauses, voice inflections, and eye contact all emphasize the attitudes and behaviors she wants the children to observe and follow. Children pay attention when adults not only express emotions nonverbally, but simultaneously talk about their feelings and the situation that caused the feelings.

Developmental Appropriateness. No matter how potent adults are as models, they cannot expect children to model behavior or attitudes that are beyond their developmental capacities. In Christine's kindergarten classroom, she is constantly stretching children's skills but is also sensitive to their limitations. Verbally and nonverbally, she acknowledges that the children may not be able to do something the way she demonstrated the first time or that they may make mistakes. As these examples have shown, one of the things Christine models is how to deal with mistakes and frustration.

Praise and Attention. Children usually remember adult behavior even when they are not rewarded for remembering. However, praise and attention may increase the likelihood that children will actually copy the behavior—as long as teachers remember that individual praise may not be consistent with the cultural values of some children's families. For example, after Christine and her student teacher had demonstrated the "spring cleaning" procedures, many of the children chose that activity during free-choice time. Christine made sure to comment specifically and warmly on the careful way in which children followed the procedures she had modeled—not just as individuals, but as a cooperative group.

COMPLEXITIES AND DIFFICULTIES IN EMOTION MODELING

The preceding suggestions sound simple. Actually, the desire to provide young children with models of emotional expression raises a number of difficult issues.

Genuineness

It is important for adults to model honest, genuine expression of emotion. However, when teachers try to apply the principle of genuineness in early education settings, they discover many complexities.

In order to be emotionally genuine, do teachers have to express their feelings exactly the same way with children as with adults? Watching Christine, one sees that she tends to be more exaggerated in her style of emotional expression when she is talking to the children than when she turns to talk to a student teacher or a parent. This phenomenon of exaggeration and "peaking" of expressive behavior is typical of how adults spontaneously communicate with young children (Malatesta-Magai, 1991). Most adults do this without even thinking about it. This does not mean the feelings are false; rather, adults seem to highlight certain aspects of their emotional communication with children, in the same way that "baby talk" spontaneously simplifies the structure of language and directs the infant's attention to important features.

But although adults typically exaggerate their emotional responses somewhat with young children, it is important that these responses not be falsified or distorted. Honest expression of adult emotion is often hard to come by in institutional settings. As Hochschild argued in *The Managed Heart* (1983), the so-called service professions sell emotion as a product. Customers in restaurants, in stores, or on airplanes are, in a sense, paying for the concern of their waiter, checkout clerk, or flight attendant. These emotions may have little relationship to the "true feelings" of the service worker. In relationships on a plane or in a restaurant, this lack of genuine emotion might be necessary and adaptive.

However, these brief, superficial relationships are very different from the more intimate and developmentally significant relationships that should exist between adults and children in early childhood settings. Yet here, too, many adults assume a bland, affectively neutral persona (Katz, 1995) or exhibit emotions that are unrelated to children's real needs. Polakow (1992) cites one example from her extended study of child care programs, in which a child deliberately and provocatively turned over a basket containing hundreds of beads. The teacher's response was to say, rather sadly and regretfully, that the child had had an accident. According to Polakow, both teacher and child knew perfectly well that it was no accident. The child was apparently trying to elicit some kind of genuine, personal emotional response from the teacher, but instead her behavior was met with a reaction that was almost bizarrely unrelated to her intentions and actions.

Appropriateness

Conflict sometimes exists between the teacher's desire to model *genuine* emotion and her desire to model the *appropriate* expression of emotion. At times, being appropriate means hiding or disguising one's true feelings. One of the most difficult tasks of teaching in an emotion-centered program is to balance emotional honesty with emotional appropriateness.

In the "weekend news" activity, Christine had decided to assign children to partners by having them match halves of puzzles she had made. Christine anticipated that some children might not be eager to do the activity with their assigned partner, and she humorously used this possibility to model appropriate responses. "What if I don't get the partner I want?" she said to the class in mock exasperation. "What if I don't get my best friend? What if I get *Patty* [the hapless student teacher] instead?" Christine wrinkled her face in an exaggerated expression of disgust. "Do I say, 'Eeeooww, not *Patty*! I don't want *Patty* for my partner!'?" Patty and the children giggled. "No," Christine continued, "I'm not going to say that, because Patty is my classmate, and I don't want to hurt my classmate's feelings. So I match my puzzle piece to Patty's"—here Christine demonstrated with a smile and an arm draped over Patty's shoulder—"and we tell our weekend news to each other."

In this example, Christine's modeling emphasized appropriateness over emotional genuineness. However, her modeling acknowledged that children might dislike their assigned partner, and she implicitly validated their right to their own feelings. Christine did not preach an emotionally dishonest message that "we all love one another in this class." Instead, her humorously modeled demonstration emphasized the hurtful consequences of expressing dislike for another child and stressed children's solidarity with their *classmates* (a term Christine uses frequently throughout the year). This group solidarity includes avoiding actions that will deliberately hurt classmates' feelings.

This example shows one way that one teacher dealt with the dilemma of genuineness and appropriateness in one situation. Influenced by a number of factors, including the age of the children, educational philosophy, personal style, and even the time of year, other early childhood professionals might choose a different balance between modeling genuineness and modeling appropriateness.

Anger Modeling

Managing anger constructively is an important developmental task for young children. One of the ways children accomplish this task is by observing how adults express and talk about anger. Outside of the early childhood program, many children are exposed to inappropriate models for anger expression. Some may live in families where anger is expressed by shouting, throwing objects, and hitting. Alcohol and drug abuse may further increase the violence of anger expression in these families. Other parents may never show anger themselves and may disapprove of or actively punish any expression of anger by their children. Through modeling, early childhood teachers can provide important, constructive alternatives to these extremes.

However, modeling the expression of anger is a complex, difficult task. Although conscientious teachers avoid deliberately frightening children with excessive displays of anger, it is not easy to maintain a balance between allowing children to experience a model of honest anger and overwhelming them with inappropriate, poorly controlled emotion.

Some early childhood teachers assiduously avoid any show of anger, believing that it is inappropriate and potentially harmful in early childhood programs. Others are more relaxed about expressing anger and feel that a certain amount of "letting loose" tends to clear the air (Hyson & Lee, 1996). Some of these differences are related to the underlying theories of emotional development discussed in Exploration 1 in Part II.

Whatever their beliefs, all adults who work with young children become genuinely angry at times. In order to model anger constructively, teachers need to prevent excessive, inappropriate outbursts of anger. Identifying situations that may trigger excessive anger is a helpful first step. Some teachers recognize that whining children cause them to lose patience. Some feel themselves becoming irrationally angry when a small child defies them; others find that unprovoked aggression arouses aggressive feelings. Teachers who are meticulous planners may find that they react angrily when children reject the activities they carefully set up. Teachers also report that certain times of the day may find them with shorter fuses than usual. Clean-up and the transition to nap time are often mentioned. Holiday periods, with special events and schoolwide assemblies, may tax patience even further, especially for teachers with family responsibilities.

Simplifying the classroom environment helps some teachers maintain an appropriate level of emotional control. For example, materials that need little supervision and that are calming for children, such as play dough or simple collage work, may reduce tension. Allowing longer blocks of time for activities may decrease the need to hurry children and may prevent outbursts of adult anger when children insist on their own timetables.

Because many early childhood classrooms have several teachers, staff can temporarily remove themselves from anger-provoking situations. However, if early childhood professionals repeatedly find themselves unable to control their angry feelings while working with young children, they need to discuss these feelings with a qualified professional. Some teachers may need to consider shifting to a different sort of position, helping children and families in settings that are less likely to trigger their frustration and anger.

Despite these prevention efforts, many teachers can recall times when they have expressed anger more directly and intensely than they wanted to. One teacher admits screaming at her 4-year-olds; another describes banging a book down on her desk, frightening the first graders into stunned silence. Another person remembers grabbing the arm of a child who had frequent tantrums and squeezing harder than was really necessary as she led him to the "quiet corner." Still another recalls hissing furiously at a one-year-old child who had tried to bite her, "You little monster!"

These outbursts were undoubtedly noticed and remembered by the children who observed them, in part because the behaviors were so out of character for these teachers. This does not mean that children were permanently damaged by these events, or that they will imitate the adults' angry outbursts. Fortunately, as noted in Chapter 3, children appear to develop concepts and behaviors not from single observations, but from prototypes that they construct from many repeated experiences.

Furthermore, if these teachers discussed their inappropriate behavior with the children after it occurred, they could partially counter its effects with more positive, appropriate models.

> You know, I was really angry at the noise during story time this morning, and I yelled at you. I yelled too loud, and I think it was scary for some children. I'm sorry that I did that. Teachers shouldn't yell at children. I think there are other ways that I could have let you know how I felt. Maybe I could have closed the book and waited, or maybe I could have said, "I am really upset about all this noise. No one can hear this story." If I had done that, you would have known that I was angry, but no one would have been scared by the yelling.

This kind of honest discussion provides children with a model of how to talk about anger, how to distinguish between appropriate and inappropriate expressions of anger, and how to consider the consequences of different kinds of anger-related behavior.

CONCLUSION

Modeling is an important strategy in helping children learn about emotions. In an emotion-centered program, adults consciously select aspects of emotion to model for children, and they integrate this emotion modeling into every aspect of the program. Teachers can increase the impact of their modeling by adopting the characteristics of effective adult models and by ensuring that children attend to their behavior, that children are developmentally able to produce the responses, and that children are praised for adopting the desired dispositions and behaviors.

The last section of this chapter discussed some particular difficulties and complexities of emotion modeling in early childhood programs. It examined what it means to express "genuine" emotion to young children, and it discussed how teachers decide whether to model honest, open emotions or whether to model appropriate inhibition of emotion expression. Because children need to learn how to express and cope with anger, and because anger is a fact of life in early childhood programs, teacher modeling of anger was given special attention. Differences in teacher beliefs about anger were discussed, and strategies for preventing inappropriate anger modeling were presented.

This chapter has portrayed the adult as a powerful, active force in influencing children's adoption of desired emotional patterns. However, children are not photographic plates, passively reproducing whatever flashes before them. And the goal of an emotion-centered program is not to create pint-sized clones of adult models, even if those models are as creative and personable as Christine. Emotional development is more than copying others' behavior. *Emotional regulation* includes a variety of processes children can use to modify their emotions and emotion-related behavior. Modeling is only one component in this critically important, complex task. In Chapter 5, we will watch Denise's group of 2- and 3-year-olds as they move toward developmentally and culturally appropriate regulation of emotions.

Supporting Children's Regulation of Emotions

It's late afternoon at the child care program where Denise teaches a group of 2- and 3-year-olds. Although the enrollment at this urban, predominantly African American center is large, a family atmosphere prevails.

A small girl wraps both arms around another child in an exuberant hug. She pulls her friend with her on a tour of the playground, as her friend smiles tentatively. "Yes, she's your friend, Tywana," Denise says quietly, as she loosens Tywana's grip on Arlette.

Four children are seated on a large tire swing, giggling. Rose, the director, has been showing a visitor the facilities. She comes over to play with the children for a moment. "Swing us, swing us!" the children call excitedly. Rose has everyone put their arms around each other; small hands grip T-shirts and wrists, and legs kick excitedly. As the tire swing starts to rotate and sway, Daria shakes her head doubtfully; she wants to leave. "Let's go slowly till Daria gets off," Rose tells the children, "and then we'll go a little faster. Leandra *needs* to hold on to you, Michelle [as Leandra grabs Michelle's arm and Michelle looks at her in alarm]. Hold on tight, everyone!"

A little later, Denise's children are back indoors. This end-of-day activity period is low key and calming. Music plays on a tape recorder. Tables are set with manipulative toys brought out just at this time of day, including dollhouses with small figures and furnishings. The sand table is equipped with scoops and cups, and the low blackboard in the corner has brightly colored chalks for scribbling. A carpeted area has room to play with trucks and cars. Denise helps each child get started at one activity area.

"Miss Denise!" calls Charlotte from the sand table. "He frow' it in my face!" Denise walks to the group and sits down companionably. "You need to tell him not to do that. You need to ask him politely, 'Can you put it down?'"

"Lemme pour it out, Harold, okay? Okay, Harold?" Charlotte repeats several times, pushing her face into Harold's. "No," says Harold, but he yields to Charlotte's insistence, finally letting her take his sifter. As Harold notices what everyone else is playing with, his face crumples and he starts to cry, looking pleadingly at Denise. His hand shoots out and he grabs a spoon that Eddie has been using. "Is that how you do it?" Denise asks Harold, in a tone of patient explanation. "Now what do you need to say to get it?" "Can I have that spoon, Eddie?" Harold asks. Eddie hands it over. "Now do you need a thank-you, Harold?" Denise prompts. Meanwhile, the boys in the rug area are crashing cars. "Vroom!" roars Alexander in his fiercest tone. "We're crashing up! Oh, man, you crashed! Watch out, here it comes!" The crashes become louder as voices rise. Denise moves toward the rug area, where Alexander is now banging two cars together wildly. She touches his shoulder. "You need to calm down, Alexander. Do you want to play cars some more, or do you want to do something else?" Almost with relief, Alexander allows Denise to walk with him from the rug area. They circle the room and end up at the chalkboard, where Alexander settles down to draw for a while.

Like all children their age, Denise's group expresses feelings with intensity and vigor. Denise and other early childhood professionals struggle with whether to encourage or restrict children's open expression of emotions.

At one extreme, some promote the emotional benefits of encouraging children to "let their feelings out." According to this view, angry exchanges, rough crashing, and direct expression of negative and positive feelings allow emotional catharsis. By draining off powerful, repressed impulses, children shed their emotional burdens and can develop healthier personalities.

At the other extreme are those who regard any emotions as disturbing and troublesome. They worry about children losing control and becoming victims of their own feelings. They believe children have little ability to channel their own feelings and behavior in appropriate directions. Adults, they think, have the job of suppressing emotional expressions that violate social conventions or that make adults uncomfortable.

Neither of these extremes is good for children, neither reflects contemporary research findings, and neither is the approach adopted by Denise and many other emotion-focused early childhood professionals. This chapter does not advocate either catharsis or suppression. Rather, its focus is on the *regulation* of emotions, a process by which children come to have increasing control over their own emotional responses and their effects on others, and by which children increasingly take on the emotional standards of their culture and context. Increasingly, psychologists and educators are seeing emotion regulation as essential to school readiness, mental health, social competence, adjustment to school, and academic success (Denham, 1998; Kopp, 2002; Shields et al., 2001; Thompson, 2002).

Emotion regulation is indeed a delicate balance that includes a number of important skills and dispositions. This chapter demonstrates that practitioners have many possible functions in helping children develop regulatory competence, and that practitioners differ in their beliefs about appropriate roles in this process. Using a variety of strategies, early childhood professionals can begin to construct an environment that supports appropriate emotion regulation. Without offering simplified recipes, I will show how practitioners can helpfully intervene at some especially difficult times. Finally, I will summarize the benefits that children receive as they become increasingly competent in regulating their own emotions and in influencing others' feelings in positive ways.

EMOTION REGULATION: THE DELICATE BALANCE

"The emotions did not evolve to be regulated. They evolved because of their inherently adaptive qualities." With these words, Izard and Kobak (1991, p. 305) remind us that human emotions have important purposes; they are not merely annoying, uncivilized impulses. Even negative emotions like anger, sadness, and fear serve to motivate purposeful behavior and have helped ensure the survival of the human species. But these functions do not require unbridled expression. In fact, Izard and Kobak go on to say that "anything as powerful as emotion requires regulation" (p. 318).

Like emotions themselves, emotion regulation plays an essential part in children's lives (Eisenberg, 2002; Fabes, Eisenberg, Shepard, Guthrie, & Poulin, 1999; Thompson, 1994). And, as this chapter will show, regulation comes from within children as well as through external adult influences. Emotion regulation is far more than the elimination of "bad" feelings; children use emotion regulation to maintain or enhance their positive emotions and to change their negative emotional states. Both positive and negative feelings can be heightened, suppressed, or modified to guide behavior, through processes of emotion regulation.

Emotion regulation includes a number of crucial skills and dispositions (Denham, 1998; Dunn & Brown, 1991; Saarni, 1999). Although the process is gradual and uneven, children who are developing competence in regulating their emotions are able to do the following:

- Monitor or keep in touch with their own emotional responses
- Stop themselves from showing inappropriate behavior related to strong positive or negative emotions
- Soothe themselves, distract themselves, or calm themselves down when they become highly emotionally aroused
- Change the intensity of their own emotional responses by using a variety of coping strategies
- Coordinate their feelings, thoughts, and actions to achieve important goals
- Use emotions to influence others' feelings and actions
- Follow cultural standards for the display of emotions

THE DEVELOPMENT OF EMOTION REGULATION

Although emotion regulation starts in infancy, the preschool years are critically important in developing emotion regulation and control. Exploration 2 in Part II contains additional readings and resources about these developmental changes. During these years, most children spend increasing amounts of time in group settings. These settings require children to balance their own wishes against those of others, to wait for things, to conform to routines, and to deal with others' strong emotional responses. Denise and other early childhood professionals play a central role in this process.

What Children Bring

No matter how skilled she is, however, Denise is not the sole regulator of her children's expression of emotions. Children's success or difficulty in emotion regulation has already been shaped by many factors even before the 2-year-olds enter Denise's class. Maturation of the brain and nervous system helps children to inhibit emotional expressions and delay gratification of impulses. Denise's children are better at waiting for turns on the tire swing than they were last year, in part because they are maturationally able to do so. For better or worse, children's early family experiences have already affected their regulatory competence (Gottman, Katz, & Hooven, 1996). The center where Denise works enrolls many children whose families experience great adversity. Poverty, violence, and instability of care have made it especially difficult for some of Denise's children to express their anger and sadness in flexible, adaptive ways. Some children have disabilities that have already influenced them to adopt certain strategies for coping with their own and others' emotional states (see Resource Note 5.1).

Furthermore, children's own resources help them begin to regulate their emotions long before they enter child care or preschool. Even infants soothe themselves and modulate their emotional arousal, although some children use these resources more effectively than others. Babies can turn

---

RESOURCE NOTE 5.1 Emotion Regulation and Children with Disabilities

Recent studies, as well as position statements and publications from national professional associations (Peth-Pierce, 2000; Sandall, McLean, & Smith, 2000) call attention to the complicated links between young children's disabilities and their difficulties in emotion regulation. The following are key points:

• A child does *not* automatically have problems with the regulation of emotions such as anger, sadness, fear, or joy just because the child has an identified disability.

• Certain disabilities *do* carry with them the strong possibility of emotion regulation problems. In some cases this is because of biological or neurological problems—for example, children with Down syndrome have difficulty understanding emotions but once aroused have difficulty regulating their feelings; and children with autism often experience intense distress over even small changes in their environment (Denham, 1998).

• In other cases the connection between disability status and emotion regulation is less direct. For example, a child with a visual impairment may have problems gaining the information needed to modulate her facial and vocal responses in ways that other children of the same age do because she cannot see and imitate their expressions. Similarly, a child with a hearing impairment may send exaggerated emotional signals to children who do not understand sign language, partly to compensate for having fewer ways to express himself to hearing children. A child with cerebral palsy may be having tantrums because she is unable to communicate her desire to participate in an activity.

• It's very important to consider whether some of these behavior patterns are really problems with emotion regulation, or whether they are adaptive strategies that are actually effective for some children at some times. In either case, we need to help the child learn an effective, appropriate way to communicate or express emotions.

• Consulting with a professional in early intervention, early childhood special education, or mental health, and referring to publications on this topic will help teachers better understand the challenges of emotion regulation for children with disabilities. With this understanding, teachers can design helpful classroom practices to support *all* children's emotional competence.

their heads away or even fall asleep if caregivers overstimulate them with talk and play. Infants can use thumbs and pacifiers as calming devices, allowing them to focus attention on a rattle or mobile. Many older infants and toddlers adopt a blanket or soft toy as a "transitional object" to soothe their distress or allay anxiety at separation (Gay & Hyson, 1976). In Chapter 2 we noted the value of these transitional objects in building security; here we note their value in promoting emotion regulation.

What Practitioners Believe and Can Do

So much has happened before children enter early childhood programs. What exactly *is* the role of the early childhood professional in fostering emotional regulation in young children? Little consensus exists. In surveying American and Korean teachers and program directors, Hyson and Lee (1996) found great variations in practitioners' endorsement of statements about certain emotion-related beliefs and strategies, such as, "When a child is upset, I try to put it in words"; "Teachers should 'let their feelings out' in class"; and "Children should be encouraged to display feelings openly." These variations existed within cultures as well as between cultures.

Rather than identifying one best role for teachers to adopt in supporting children's emotion regulation, it may be better to examine an array of possible roles. As recent discussions of appropriate practices and professional preparation have emphasized (Bredekamp & Copple, 1997; NAEYC, 2001), early childhood professionals need a broad repertoire of strategies to help young children learn. With skill in all of these strategies, practitioners can select those that are best suited to children's individual needs, cultural expectations, and educational purposes. When Alexander's car crashing became wild and uncontrolled, Denise had many options from which to choose. Her gentle distraction and guidance to a new activity worked effectively, but other choices were possible. Another child (or even Alexander on a different day) might have been able to regain control with a look from Denise. Simply moving closer to Alexander and the other boys might have been sufficient. On the other hand, at times Denise may need to take over the regulatory function completely, physically removing Alexander from the area and holding him firmly until his excitement and anger subside.

As practitioners try to enhance children's skills in regulating emotions, they may take on three kinds of roles: the *smorgasbord host*, the *scaffold*, and the *cultural guide*.

The Smorgasbord Host. The activities and materials in Denise's early childhood program offer children many avenues to express feelings and regulate their expression in constructive, challenging ways. Pretend play, manipulative activities, creative arts, physical activity—these and other program features are like items on a smorgasbord laid out for children's selection (Howes, 1992, has used this and the following metaphor in a slightly different context). Like the host at this feast, Denise has arranged the selection to appeal to her "guests," and like a good host, she welcomes the children to the feast and describes its specialties. She invites children to sample whatever they like, pointing out their favorites but urging them to try new items. She encourages them to return again and again to the table, pacing themselves to ensure enjoyment without overstuffing.

The Scaffold. Sometimes children need more than a host. Another role that Denise and others frequently assume is that of a helpful scaffold. The concept of "scaffolding" has been used in discussions of adults' roles in supporting cognitive development through close interaction and support as children work on emerging skills (Berk & Winsler, 1995). The concept is also useful when thinking about self regulation and early emotional development (Bodrova & Leong, 1995). Like a framework around a new building, Denise's individual interactions with children support their emerging attempts at emotion regulation. With Denise's support, children are able to maintain a higher level of emotional control than they can manage on their own. At the sand table, Denise's presence and close interaction help the children sustain their positive feelings and reduce angry exchanges.

Some may feel these techniques are too directive. However, a certain amount of adult scaffolding is needed if young children are to develop empathy, prosocial behavior, and appropriate regulation of emotions (Denham, 1998; Saarni, 1999). Rather than building dependency on Denise or other teachers, these scaffolding interactions establish emotional competencies that children are later able to use independently.

The Cultural Guide. When Sanika grabs Julius's shirt and tries to pull him off the chair, Denise firmly addresses her, "If he's in your seat, what do you need to say?" When Marcus reaches for a picture that Gloria has been examining, Denise says to him, "You ask her, 'Gloria, can I see it? Can I see that, Gloria?' That's the way you ask her, Marcus." He looks up at Denise. When she assumes this role, she is providing children with what Piaget called conventional knowledge. She calmly but directly instructs children about appropriate, socially acceptable behavior: asking permission to take things, saying please and thank you and excuse me, apologizing for hurting others. Frequently during the day, Denise will remind children of norms for the well-regulated expression of emotions.

These are not understandings that children can acquire simply through maturation. Through observation and direct instruction, children learn what kind of emotion expressions and controls are expected in various situations. Gradually, they begin to internalize these standards and to express even intense emotions in culturally consistent ways (Kitayama & Markus, 1994). "Don't say that word!" says Eddie to Alexander. "That's right," says Denise. "It's not nice to talk to your friends that way."

Compared with some other teachers of this age group, Denise places an especially high priority on acquiring cultural display rules for emotions and on adopting patterns of emotion-related behavior valued by the African American community that the center serves. This knowledge does more than help children be polite. Children who are familiar with accepted emotional display rules are more likely to become socially competent (Jones, Abbey, & Cumberland, 1998). In studies of parents' beliefs and attitudes (Hale-Benson, 1986; McAdoo, 1997), African American families have consistently valued children's early adherence to adult social conventions. In her calm, encouraging style, Denise is guiding her children not just toward general cultural standards, but also into patterns of emotion regulation that are consistent with specific family and community expectations. Yet she does so in the context of a classroom environment where children are kissed, hugged, and encouraged to express their feelings in a lively, physical way.

AN ENVIRONMENT FOR EMOTION REGULATION

Using the roles of smorgasbord host, scaffold, and cultural guide, early childhood professionals can construct an environment within which children can strengthen their abilities to regulate their own emotions and to respond appropriately to others' feelings.

Establishing the Interpersonal Climate

The strategies presented in earlier chapters help children build regulatory skills: creating a secure emotional environment; helping children understand their own feelings and those of others; and serving as a model of genuine, appropriate emotion expressions. A positive interpersonal climate will also support the development of emotion regulation.

Children who are in "good moods" are more likely to tune in to others' feelings, to be generous to others, and to help those in trouble (Moore, 1985). Denise's class and other high quality programs are happy places for children and adults. Despite conflicts among children and occasional reprimands for misbehavior, the dominant mood is positive and loving. Rose, the director of Denise's program, says that the first thing many visitors comment on is how happy everyone seems to be. Staff turnover is low. Foster grandparents, parent helpers, and other community volunteers enjoy being around the center; children who have graduated to public school come back to visit. Children bask in the warmth of the center's nurturing extended family.

Although she instructs children in culturally valued patterns of regulation, Denise matter-of-factly and openly accepts children's expression of a wide variety of emotions. She assumes that young children will express anger, excitement, and distress; they will cry, hit each other, grab toys, and squeal with joy. Denise does not express horror or dismay at any of this; rather, she starts with children's present level of behavior and moves them toward desired patterns of appropriate expression. This kind of open affective exchange sets the stage for the development of empathy and healthy emotion regulation (Denham, 1998; Eisenberg & Fabes, 1992a).

We have already seen that talking about emotions helps children understand their own and others' feelings. "Feeling-talk" is equally important in emotion regulation. Children who do not learn to use emotion language have a hard time making connections with their own feelings and accurately identifying how others feel; this deficit places them at increased risk for emotion-regulation problems. Denise weaves emotion language into many of her interactions: "You need to calm down," she comments, as Alexander roars and crashes his cars. Later, in a concerned tone Denise observes, "You're hurting your babies," as two children bang dolls on the floor. However, a warning is in order: Not all talk about feelings is conducive to healthy emotion regulation. Cicchetti and colleagues observe that some adults use language to overintellectualize or distance themselves from their own and others' feelings, and that their children may end up with maladaptive patterns of emotion regulation (Cicchetti, Ganiban, & Barnett, 1991).

Adults support the regulation of emotion if they help children see that they can change their own negative feelings or can help others feel better. When Harold was upset because he wanted Eddie's spoon, Denise showed him how he could control his distress and negotiate the situation in a satisfying way. Such experiences build children's feelings of self-efficacy—an important outcome of positive emotional development (Saarni, 1999).

Emotion regulation is also supported in a climate where children focus on other people. Coordinating one's own desires with those of others is impossible unless one is aware of others' feelings and unless one genuinely cares about the effect one's behavior has on others. Children like the 2- and 3-year-olds in Denise's class do not automatically come to this awareness. Adult involvement—and adult coaching—are essential (Eisenberg & Fabes, 1998; Thompson, 2002). Denise has qualities that research has found effective in creating this awareness of others' feelings and needs: She is highly nurturant in her interactions with children, and she uses induction or reasoning as a discipline strategy, explicitly directing children's attention to the consequences of their behavior for others. "He doesn't like it when you ask him that way," Denise said gently, with a restraining hand on Eddie.

Promoting Peer Interactions

So far we have focused on the adult-child interpersonal climate. But peer interactions give children an especially potent setting to learn about regulating emotions. Children are powerful influences on one another's social competence, in both positive and negative directions (Denham et al., 2001). And because other children are often less tolerant than adults of unpleasant emotional displays (Kopp, 1989), classmates may simply refuse to play with children who lack emotional control. This is a powerful though painful incentive for children to gain skill at modulating their anger, distress, and excitement.

Playing with others also helps children learn how to influence or regulate others' emotional states. In Denise's class, Raymond has become skilled at raising other children's interest in his games: "Come on, doggy," he begs, panting and hanging his tongue out of his mouth as he wheedles two other children to join in his play. "We're the doggies, right?" Enticed by his expressions and playful actions, the others woof enthusiastically and join in.

Providing Activities

The emotion-centered teacher knows that classroom activities can help children learn to monitor, heighten, dampen, redirect, and otherwise regulate their expressive behavior. Many of the best activities allow children to represent their experiences, encouraging feelings of efficacy or control.

Observing Denise's children, one can see how they use the program's activities to build emotion regulation skills. Just as it supports emotional understanding, pretend play is important for the regulation of emotions (Bodrova & Leong, 2003). Dunn and Brown (1991) found that toddlers used more emotion language and were more engaged in expressing emotions during make-believe play than at any other time. And preschoolers who engage more often in pretend play, especially with a more skilled play partner, are better able to regulate their emotions, even in other contexts (Galyer & Evans, 2001).

In pretend play, children can experiment with intense feelings. In Denise's room, Tywana and Arlette lay on their backs, pretending to sleep, eyes squinched tight. Teasingly, Eddie rolled a truck into them. In mock fear, they "woke up," shrieked loudly, and fled to the book corner, where they huddled with their arms around each other, smiling gleefully. These kinds of episodes let children practice expressing a great range of emotions through words, gestures, and symbolic actions, turning them on and off at will.

Like pretend play, painting and other creative activities not only provide emotional outlets , but also give children access to additional, culturally valued ways of expressing feelings. Denise makes particularly effective use of music throughout her program. During a period when the children are in small groups using manipulative materials, Denise turns on a lively, familiar tape. As they stand at small tables working on puzzles and Lego structures, most of the children move in time to the music, performing little spontaneous dances. At one point, Bradley takes Whitney's hand and dances on the rug, returning to his table a few minutes later. Rather than distracting them from their "work," the emotional and physical satisfactions of music seem to focus the children's attention and heighten their enjoyment.

All these activities extend children's capacities for emotion regulation. Through pretending, drawing, dancing, building, swinging, and many other symbolic and physical activities, children build a repertoire of options for expressing, exaggerating, and minimizing emotions, and for coordinating their feelings with others. This broad repertoire sets the stage for emotional competence (see Resource Note 5.2).

INTERVENTIONS AT DIFFICULT TIMES

It is not easy for young children to regulate their emotions, and certain situations make it even harder. A child lashes out angrily at a classmate; children tease or reject others; a child's fears are aroused in a new situation; children have to wait for something they really want—these and other challenging encounters call for skilled adult intervention.

RESOURCE NOTE 5.2 What Are You Doing to Help Children
Develop Emotion-Regulation Skills?

Early childhood professionals have recommended the following strategies for adults to use in helping children appropriately regulate their expressions of emotions:

• I make it a priority to establish a loving, secure relationship with each child in my class.
• I help children learn about feelings, their own and others'.
• I try to serve as a model for genuine, appropriate expressions of emotion.
• I create a positive climate in my program—children are happy and relaxed most of the time.
• I openly acknowledge children's feelings (even if they are not well regulated right now) and work with children over time to move toward greater regulation.
• I help children to use emotion words as part of their overall language development.
• I help children see how to change their own emotional responses or help others feel better, thus giving them a greater sense of efficacy or control.
• I direct children's attention to others' feelings and needs.
• I create many opportunities for peer play where children learn to regulate their emotions to keep the play going.
• I promote close friendships among children, because it is easier to begin to regulate emotions with people you care deeply about.
• I offer many activities that allow children to represent their feelings acceptably through pretend play, art, writing, movement, and other media.

When Children Face Another's Anger

Children differ greatly in their responses to another child's anger or aggression. Some quickly seek revenge, while others shrink back and avoid any conflict. Many teachers agree that an assertive response is the most desirable—standing up for one's rights without losing control completely. Eisenberg and Fabes (1992b) found that adults' responses to children's negative emotions predicted how children would react to other children's anger. As one might expect, those who punish their children's negative emotion, or who minimize its importance, are more likely to have children who seek revenge when angered or who avoid the aggressor completely. Adults who respond to their children's distress by taking it seriously (but not punishing it) tend to have children who can regulate their own anger better in response to peer aggression. Although the adults in this study were parents, not teachers, the results have implications for early childhood professionals. Denise does not ignore or laugh off children's anger and distress, but neither does she react in shock and anger. Her attitude may help explain the low levels of aggression observed among her young children, despite their frequent conflicts.

When Children Hurt Others' Feelings

One of Denise's children, Phylicia, has an observable physical disability. Staring and teasing about Phylicia's appearance are not allowed in Denise's class, although Denise calmly and matter-of-factly answered children's questions at the beginning of the year. Some practitioners may believe that natural expressions of emotion should never be discouraged, and that children will come to think curiosity is a bad thing if they are discouraged from staring and commenting. But studies of the development of prosocial behavior indicate that Denise's prohibitions are helpful. Parents who explicitly instruct their children to control emotional displays that could be hurtful to others (such as staring at a person with a disability) tend to have more sympathetic children (Eisenberg & Valiente, 2002). Such prohibitions do not restrict children from any and all emotional displays—only those that hurt others' feelings.

When Children Are Anxious

All children have fears (Hyson, 1979). Adults can easily understand some of these fears (fear of injections, hospitals, violence), while others are harder to comprehend (fear of Halloween masks, balloons, new hairdos). Helping children deal with anxiety-producing situations is a complex process. Some children's fears are intense and disabling enough to require expert consultation. With more routine fears, adults need to assist children in two areas: coping with the event and regulating their level of fear and anxiety.

In Denise's class, a grandparent once hired someone to dress up as Big Bird to help celebrate a child's birthday. To the grandparent's surprise, many children were distressed by the unexpected appearance of their formerly favorite character. What might have helped? As adults, we often want children to face up to issues—including Big Bird—squarely. But emotion regulation may be better served with a gradual, indirect process. Concrete demonstrations or modeling can help (for example, a puppet demonstration before Big Bird's surprise appearance). Or the teacher might focus the children's attention away from the unexpected features of the situation and onto more familiar aspects—the Big Bird visitor's resemblance to pictures in one of their storybooks. All these approaches can help children regulate their negative emotional responses through increased control and distraction (Denham, 1998).

When Children Have to Wait

Denise's young preschoolers have a hard time waiting for their snack. Seated at tables and hearing food carts being trundled to other classrooms, they can quickly lose control, with contagious whining filling the room. Denise, like other effective early childhood teachers, minimizes useless waiting time as much as she can, but in any group setting some waiting is unavoidable. Waiting calls on children's ability to control or manage their emotional states, and the ability to delay gratification is an important index of emotional competence (Sethi, Mischel, Aber, Shoda, & Rodriguez, 2000).

Children cope most effectively with the frustration and anxiety of waiting when they can avoid thinking about what they are waiting for or when they can imaginatively transform it in some way (Moore, 1985). Giving children something else to occupy their time while they wait is especially effective; Denise has found that simply giving each child a sheet of paper and a crayon creates a distraction that helps them keep their presnack distress under control (and produces some wonderful scribbles besides).

Children's emotional states also influence their ability to delay gratification. Once again, the happy mood of Denise's classroom creates advantages in the development of emotion regulation, at the same time that it makes it easier for her children to wait for what they want.

BENEFITS OF REGULATION

Emotion regulation is not easy, but it has significant benefits. When children increase their ability to monitor or modify their own emotional responses, learn appropriate display rules, and influence others' emotional states in positive, flexible, culturally accepted ways, at least five benefits result:

1. *Children reach the goals they desire.* Getting what one wants, whether it is a snack, a friend, or completion of a task, requires successful emotion regulation. Too much distress or fearfulness, for example, can inhibit children from exploring and can restrict their later cognitive and social development. Emotion regulation puts children's feelings to work, helping children reach their goals.
2. *Children feel better.* Overwhelming emotion, both negative and positive, can cause confusion and a scary sense of being out of control. Children feel better when they know that they have some control over how they feel and how they express it (sometimes with a lot of adult scaffolding), and when they are confident that others will take their feelings seriously.
3. *Children experience mastery.* Healthy development requires a sense of competence and mastery. Many accomplishments contribute to this sense, but an especially important one is children's confidence that they can use their emotions in ways of their choosing and in ways that others value.
4. *Children become part of the culture.* Because norms for regulating emotions are culturally defined, children who are skilled in emotion regulation become increasingly integrated into their culture. They are accepted as functioning members of the community, who share the standards others have set.
5. *Children become more socially competent.* Emotion regulation contributes to peer acceptance and social competence. In families and in early childhood programs, children constantly encounter others whose emotional thresholds and needs differ from their own. Children must learn to modify their own expressions of emotion and direct their attention to others' feelings.

CONCLUSION

The process of developing emotion-regulation skills is increasingly recognized as one of the most important dimensions of school readiness and later academic and social competence. It is also extremely complex, much more so than this short chapter can convey. Early childhood professionals need to be creative and flexible if they are to help with this process, and at times they need the extra help of mental health professionals or intensive interventions (see Resource Note 5.3). Denise and other teachers know that children need different kinds of support at different times. One child may need to experience a kind of emotional release after a traumatic experience; another may need to retreat for a while through simple pretend

---

RESOURCE NOTE 5.3 When Children Can't Regulate Their Emotions

The suggestions in this chapter will support emotion regulation in most situations and with most children. However, some children have difficulties that go far beyond what is typical for their age—for example, Sandra reacts to any minor disappointment with deep sadness, weeping, and withdrawal; and Amos's physical aggression is increasing, directed against the youngest and most vulnerable children. Because emotion dysregulation carries risks for later problems in other areas of social, emotional, cognitive, and academic development, these difficulties should not be ignored. The following are some steps that could be taken:

• Systematic observation of when and how a child shows emotion-regulation problems is always needed, both in designing classroom-based interventions and in discussing the problems with family members or other professionals. Assessment tools like those in Appendix D can help focus the observations on the most significant behaviors.

• Classroom-based interventions developed specifically for children with serious emotion regulation difficulties may help. Appendix B describes some such programs.

• Communication with families is essential, to gain a sense of whether the difficulties are seen at home as well as at school, and to plan a consistent approach to helping the child. Cultural respect and understanding are important, as children's behaviors or intervention strategies that may be acceptable in one culture may be less acceptable and less effective in another (Lynch & Hanson, 1998).

• Referrals for further assessment by mental health or other professionals are often essential. Depending on the nature of the difficulties, more than one profession may be involved, always with a team approach in mind. These assessments will provide added information that can be used to develop a collaborative plan to increase the child's ability to regulate emotions. The plan might begin with a focused classroom intervention but could, if needed, include individual or group therapy, family counseling, medication, or a combination of these. It's always best to begin with a less-intrusive intervention, assessing its effectiveness over time.

• Some early childhood programs have the regular services of a mental health consultant with special training in early childhood education, who functions as a member of the team in meeting children's needs. This service is one that many professionals believe should be available to every program, but too often is not (Raver & Knitzer, 2002).

---

play or sensory activities. Many children simply need gentle guidance to extend and broaden their ways of expressing emotions. At times, others need explicit instruction in a warm atmosphere. We try to socialize children to conform to the norms of their culture, but we also recognize that young children are not able to adhere to those norms consistently.

This chapter has mentioned but not fully explored individual differences in children's styles of expressing and regulating emotions. In Chapter 6, Hope's class will show us the many ways in which early childhood professionals can recognize and honor these expressive styles.

Recognizing and Honoring Children's Expressive Styles

Hope has made copies of a poem for her multiage primary class. It is titled "tiger":

The tiger
Has swallowed
A black sun.

In his cold
Cage he
Carries it still:

Black flames
Flicker through
His fur,

Black rays roar
From the centers
Of his eyes.

Valerie Worth, *Small Poems Again* (1975, 1986)

As Hope passes out copies of the poem, she says to the children, "This poem has been very controversial at my house. My son Will, who is 17, said to me, 'Your class will *never* understand this.'" At that, Serena rolls her eyes at Will's obtuseness. Hope continues. "And one of the other teachers looked at the poem when I was copying it. She said to me, 'Wow, that's an exciting poem, but it's pretty *dark*, isn't it?' But, you know, I think there are some interesting ideas in this poem—about animals' feelings and about our respect for animals."

Hope reads the poem aloud twice, as the children follow along. She guides a group discussion of the poem, helping the children put their feelings and understanding into words. In the discussion, Hope gently encourages quieter children to contribute. Kathy's soft answer, "Maybe the tiger doesn't want anyone to look at him in the zoo," illuminates both the poem and Kathy's own emotional style. Other children describe seeing animals in the zoo, and they respond to Hope's questions about how the tiger might feel "in his cold cage." Following the discussion, the children read the poem by themselves, using markers to highlight the words they are sure of—a routine the class follows with all poems to be included in their notebooks.

As the children work, Hope moves around the room, watching what the children are doing, answering questions, and providing help. She leans over Federico, who is sitting looking at his paper. Federico's family speaks Spanish at home, and he continues to need some extra support as he builds his reading and writing skills in English. Hope points to the first line. "Federico, I bet you know this word." "*The,*" Federico whispers, picking up his marker. "And how about that word?" Hope questions. "*Sun,*" says Federico with a stronger voice.

After the children work individually on the poem, they each draw a picture to illustrate it. Azra laboriously copies a picture from a nature book on the shelf. "You found a good book to help you there, Azra," Hope says. Serena's tiger has bold stripes, large pointed teeth, and a fierce expression. "Now *that's* a tiger, Serena!" Hope exclaims. Serena grins and nods proudly.

As the morning goes on, the children work in small groups reading "tiger" and old favorite poems to each other. Xavier waits alone on the rug. "Xavier," Hope says with gentle humor and confidence, "I think you have to get up and be a little more active, to find someone who wants you for a partner. Somebody will!" As the children read poems together, Hope listens in. Some children read fluently and exuberantly; others hesitate over each word as if worried about making a mistake. Some children quickly select poems to read, while others leaf slowly through their notebooks before making a decision.

Later, the class gathers on the rug to read their own writing and to talk with Hope about the "tiger" poem and other stories with tiger themes. At the end of the discussion, Hope sums up: "You have all worked really hard this morning." "Whew!" calls Mario loudly. "Can we have recess?" Hope and the others laugh and nod in shared satisfaction.

During the morning, the children in Hope's class worked on some common tasks: They read a poem, they drew pictures, they found partners to read together, they wrote stories, and they discussed one another's work in progress. Yet although they all were working on the same things, the children showed striking individual differences in how they approached these tasks and how they showed their feelings about their work, themselves, and their classmates.

If you ask any early childhood teacher to describe the children in her class, the chances are that she will use emotion words. Federico is "quiet" and "shy"; Serena is "exuberant" and "proud"; Xavier is "cautious" and "hesitant." To create an emotion-centered program, teachers must recognize and honor these individual differences in children's emotional expressiveness. This chapter will help teachers focus more closely on emotion-related individual differences. It will also suggest strategies that allow teachers to observe these differences more carefully and to keep track of their observations. I will underscore the importance of respecting and honoring children's unique expressive styles. The chapter will end by acknowledging some obstacles to teachers' acceptance of these emotional patterns.

WHAT IS EXPRESSIVENESS AND WHERE DOES IT COME FROM?

Defining Expressiveness

Expressiveness can be defined as a persistent individual style of emotional response (Denham, Lehman, Moser, & Reeves. 1995; Halberstadt, 1991; Malatesta, Culver, Tesman, & Shepard, 1989). Emotions are universal: Children and adults all over the world experience and express basic emotions such as joy, anger, sadness, and interest. However, the children in Hope's class—and people everywhere—also have uniquely different patterns or styles of emotional responsiveness. For example, as the children worked on their illustrations of the tiger poem, they all seemed to experience the emotion of interest. But children showed their feelings in very different ways. Serena's whole body reflected her absorption in the task, and she eagerly sought others with whom to share her pleasure at her accomplishment. Peter, in contrast, shut others out, hunching over his drawing in solitary absorption. Azra's interest was sporadic and diffused. Once she found a book to copy from, she involved herself in the task, but before that she sat at the table gazing off into the distance and wandered around the room, looking at what others were doing.

Sources of Expressive Styles

These individual differences, like other aspects of emotional development, are neither entirely inborn nor entirely learned. Halberstadt (1991) describes *expressive styles* as complex individual patterns of emotional communication. These styles develop gradually over time, as a product of biological, cultural, and social influences. Thus children become more different from one another the older they get. Federico and Serena were probably more similar as babies than they are today. But if one had known Serena as an infant, one might already have seen some indications of the expressive style she displays as an 8-year-old. Her genetic inheritance may have predisposed her to a highly sociable disposition and to an easy readiness to smile and laugh.

However, her family environment also shaped the precise direction taken by Serena's individual expressive style. Her family, although warm and loving, is not highly expressive. Like many young children from "low expressive families" (Halberstadt, Crisp, & Eaton, 1999), Serena readily expresses positive emotions but is slow to express anger. Serena's parents have little tolerance for children's expressions of anger. Serena's parents do not go along with the idea that children should "let their feelings out." Partly because of their unique family expressive style, and partly because of their Puerto Rican cultural norms (Miller & Harwood, 2001), they actively discourage the expression of negative emotions toward adults. The cultural value of "proper demeanor" or respectful behavior is emphasized in Serena's family from infancy onward.

By the time Serena reached Hope's class, then, her expressive style was well formed. Over the past year, Serena has further developed her unique style, in part because Hope's program has given her many opportunities. As one of the oldest children in this mixed-age class, Serena has been able to see herself as a guide and model for the younger children. This has certainly influenced her way of expressing her feelings and her emotional responses to classroom activities.

Finally, we need to recognize that children may show their unique emotional patterns differently in different situations. When Serena is on the playground or helping her father work on their house, she shows the same typical expressive patterns as she does when she is working on a tiger picture in the classroom. But there *are* differences in how she shows her feelings, depending on the specific social context. Even as a primary-grade child, she is already learning the display rules of her family's culture and those of the wider culture of which she is also a part, and she is able to modify her own expressive style to meet the expectations of varied social settings.

HOW TO RECOGNIZE CHILDREN'S EXPRESSIVE STYLES

The more attuned a teacher is to the unique emotional response patterns of young children, the better able she will be to use this information in building a positive, emotion-centered program.

Identifying Basic Emotions

Before early childhood professionals are able to create detailed pictures of individual children's expressive styles, they need to be sure they are able to make accurate judgments about basic emotion expressions and emotion-related behavior.

Facial expressions give clear clues about emotions. For example, a researcher looking at a videotape of Federico would probably judge that he was feeling both sad and a little shy. The judgment would be based on several observations: Federico's mouth is downturned, his eyes are not as bright as usual, and his face and body seem droopy. He seems to be comforting himself by thumbsucking. As Hope approaches, Federico's shyness may be evident when he turns his head away and avoids looking at his teacher. As Hope helps Federico to become more confident about identifying the words he knows in the tiger poem, signs of interest appear: Federico's brows are lifted, his eyes brighten, and his mouth relaxes and opens slightly. His posture shifts from its helpless slump, and he picks up the marker, exploring the paper with his hand and his eyes. Although most early childhood educators would have little interest in or time for this microlevel analysis, practitioners who are aware of the basic facial and bodily expressions of emotion will be more able to appreciate differences among children's expressive styles.

Looking for Dimensions of Difference

What makes Serena's style so different from Federico's? Halberstadt (1991) described six dimensions on which children's expressiveness may differ:

1. *Balance of positive and negative emotions.* Everyone experiences both positive and negative emotions, but people differ in how frequently they experience and express these feelings. Federico's general mood, for example, is much more frequently negative

than is Phoebe's. Serena's expressive style is consistently positive; on the rare occasions when she shows sadness or anger, Hope wonders if she is coming down with a cold or if some problem has occurred at home.

2. *Frequency of specific emotion displays.* Children have consistent differences in how often they show more specific emotions. Xavier frequently displays fear and shyness, being inhibited in new situations, especially social ones. Phoebe is notable for her frequent expressions of joy; of all the children in Hope's class, she is the one who most often claps her hands, giggles in delight, and smiles broadly at any pleasurable experience.

3. *Intensity of emotion expressions.* Two children who are alike in their frequency of expressing an emotion such as anger may be very different in the intensity with which they show these feelings. Neither Peter nor Azra is often angry, but when Peter is upset he explodes in a rage, stomping about and yelling at anyone who gets in his way. Azra, on the other hand, shows her anger in a more muted way: She may sit at her desk, hands clenched and eyes narrowed, glaring at the person who has offended her. When Hope surprised the children with a new math game, Serena's eyes widened slightly and she drew in her breath in anticipation, while Randall struck himself on the forehead and flopped on the rug in an exaggerated pantomime of astonishment.

4. *Duration of specific emotional states.* In Hope's class as in other early childhood settings, some children shift quickly from one emotional state to another. Upset by a classmate's rejection, Azra's tears quickly turn to smiles when another child invites her to play. Other children, like Peter, are more likely to persist in sadness or anger. At the end of the day, Peter stood at the door, shaking his head disconsolately. When Hope asked him what was the matter, she found out that he was still thinking about an incident on the playground at morning recess, when Adam would not let him have the ball.

5. *Pure versus mixed emotion expressions.* Children's faces are fascinating to watch. Although all children use more blended emotion expressions as they get older, there are strong individual differences in how often children display these "mixed" feelings in comparison to more direct, "pure" emotion expressions. In Hope's class, everyone always knows exactly how Leo is feeling. His face is a mirror of basic emotions. When he is happy, his expression is almost a classic vision of joy; and when he is angry, every line on his face and every muscle in his body shows that single emotion. In contrast, Federico's face and body typically reflect more complicated combinations of feelings. His happiness is often mixed with shyness, and interest and sadness seem to alternate on his face as he tackles the challenges of schoolwork.

6. *Speed of emotion onset*. Finally, expressive differences are seen in how quickly children's emotions are activated. The whole class laughed at Mario's demand for recess, but the children did not all start laughing at once. Rachel's giggles were heard first (as they usually are in Hope's room), while it took a little time for Leo to join in. Similarly, when Hope began reading "tiger," some children were immediately fascinated by the poem, leaning forward in a posture of complete emotional engagement. Others took longer to be drawn in, their interest expressions only becoming evident during Hope's second reading.

These dimensions of difference may be very helpful in focusing on the unique emotional characteristics of the young children you teach. Resource Note 6.1 offers some questions to get you started.

TOOLS FOR IDENTIFYING EMOTIONAL STYLES

Teachers can use a number of relatively simple tools to focus on individual expressive styles. At the same time, these tools will give teachers greater insight into other, interconnected aspects of their children's development and learning.

Classroom Organization and Activities

To learn about children's styles, teachers must work in an environment that allows them to step back occasionally and just "kidwatch." A program like Hope's makes this possible. From the very beginning of the year, Hope has encouraged children to do things for themselves. Long periods each day are spent in independent work. Classroom helpers (Recess Equipment Manager, Chalkboard Specialist) take care of many routine housekeeping chores. Supplies are readily available. Older children help their younger classmates with reading and math work. Besides building security and self-esteem, these management strategies give Hope some solid blocks of time in which she can really look at what children are doing and how they are doing it.

The activities provided in Hope's program also make children's individual expressive styles much more apparent. Because children have many choices, their selections can tell Hope and other observers a great deal. Even when all the children are doing the same activity, the activity can usually be done in many different ways. In planning a drawing activity, some teachers might give children a predrawn tiger picture to fill in with prescribed colors. Hope chose a different and more productive strategy. Following the earlier group discussion and small group work, she invited the children to "draw a picture of how the poem makes you feel." The

RESOURCE NOTE 6.1 The Dimensions of Difference

As you look at the children in your class, consider the many ways in which they are different in their emotion styles—not better, not worse, just different.

- *Positive and negative emotional balance*
    Who is always upbeat?
    Who's usually neutral?
    Who goes around a bit downcast much of the time?
    Who swings from one extreme to another?
- *Showing specific emotions*
    Who is your most fearful child?
    Who's most likely to show anger?
    Who always looks surprised when something new happens?
- *Emotion intensity*
    Whose emotions are the most vivid or intense (positive or negative)?
    Whose feelings seem the most low key and subtle?
- *Length or duration of emotion expression*
    When the group gets excited about a new activity, whose excitement lasts the longest?
    When an argument breaks out on the playground, whose annoyance takes the longest to settle down?
- *One emotion versus a combination*
    Whose feelings often seem to be a complex mixture—a bit of fear, a bit of excitement, a bit of sadness, a bit of interest?
    And whose emotions are generally unmixed—100% happy or 100% angry?
- *Speed of emotion activation*
    Who is the first to jump up with excitement when a baby sister is brought to school?
    Who takes the longest to react when the class finds out that the trip to the zoo has to be cancelled?

There are no right answers here: These and other questions will help you take a closer look at the children in your care, to understand and appreciate the unique combination of emotion styles that make them—and you—the people you are.

children's individual drawings provided a fascinating glimpse of their unique emotional styles.

Some activities are almost guaranteed to highlight differences in expressive styles. Inspired by spring weather, robins, and a recent rainy spell, Hope's class has been studying worms. One afternoon was spent inspecting worms that Hope had obtained for the class. After a group discussion (including the development of humane guidelines for handling the worms), each child was given a worm to observe closely, using a magnifying glass.

The children were encouraged to write notes for their science notebooks. Every emotion imaginable could be observed on children's faces, in their voices, and in their bodies. Azra gently touched her worm, stroking it and smiling as the worm moved across the paper. Leo stretched out a tentative finger, yanking it back before even touching his worm, and looking anxiously at his friend Jeremy, who attended to his worm with scientific precision, writing his notes in careful printing.

Observation Methods

Early childhood educators have traditionally valued well-recorded observations of children's behavior. Recently, many psychologists who are interested in early emotional development have followed this tradition, observing naturally occurring behavior in home, community, and school settings. A small but growing number of researchers have begun to observe children's emotional development in child care centers and other early childhood programs (e.g., Denham et al., 1995; Fabes, Hanish, Martin, & Eisenberg, 2002; Garner & Spears, 2000; Walter & LaFreniere, 2000).

Note Taking. Many early childhood educators have been trained in writing anecdotal records. The challenge is not how to do it, but rather, making the time to do it. Hope has devised a note-taking system that uses the large blank address labels that come on a long continuous paper roll. She has found that these are easy to jot notes on as she moves around the room visiting small groups of children and as children conference with her about their reading and writing. She uses these sticky labels to note many aspects of children's behavior, including their emotional responses to classroom activities. The labels can then be peeled off their backing and added to the individual folders Hope keeps for the children in the class.

The growth of interest in authentic, classroom-based assessment, portfolios, work sampling, documentation, and other naturalistic approaches to assessing children's progress has spurred the development of numerous resources. These offer teachers realistic suggestions for taking notes in the classroom and for organizing these observations (Grace & Shores, 1994; High/Scope Staff, 1992; McAfee & Leong, 2002; Meisels et al., 1995). No one system is best; the point is to find one that works and use it regularly.

Videotaping Children. Because so much of children's emotional life is communicated through facial expression, gesture, and body movement, videotape offers a medium that is well matched to the teacher's need for appropriate observational tools. Our expanded knowledge about early emotional development can be attributed in part to researchers' use of sophisticated video technology to record and review examples of children's expression of feelings.

A growing number of schools and child care programs now have access to portable video cameras. Teachers can learn a great deal about children by watching them on videotape. Subtle patterns of emotion that are lost in the bustle of the classroom may take on new significance when they are reviewed at the end of the day or in a weekly staff meeting; and again, the same videotapes will give useful insight into language and literacy development, mathematical competence, social skills, and other important outcomes for children.

Videotaping is not as complicated as the newcomer may fear, and practical advice is available about this and related forms of documentation (Helm, Beneke, & Steinheimer, 1997). The hardest thing is getting started. If there are two teachers in the room (or if a parent volunteer can be recruited), one teacher can videotape on a regular basis (perhaps once a week). Even with only one adult, programs organized like Hope's have some periods of time when children can easily work independently.

What should be videotaped? Almost anything will provide useful information, but tapes of children working on open-ended, emotion-laden activities are especially revealing. A visitor to Hope's class happened to videotape the children's worm observations; the resulting tape offers an inexhaustibly rich resource for understanding individual children's emotions. One school enlists a parent volunteer to tape each child twice a year, during several kinds of activities. The tapes are saved for the 3 or 4 years that most children are enrolled, providing a fascinating archive of developmental and individual information for staff and parents.

Emotion-Related Scales and Checklists. Another useful observational tool is an emotion-related scale or checklist. Resource Note 6.2 and Appendix D describe a number of teacher-friendly observation scales and checklists that include items focused on individual differences in emotional expressiveness, as well as differences in emotion expression and regulation. As with any such tools, it is important to use these as one of many assessment approaches, arriving at a richer and more accurate picture of children's strengths and needs. Position statements and guidelines for appropriate uses of early childhood assessment tools are helpful in weighing how and when to use these (Meisels & Atkins-Burnett, 2002, NAEYC & NAECS/SDE, 2003).

USING KNOWLEDGE OF EXPRESSIVE STYLES

Knowledge is of little value unless it can be used. Teachers who take the time to organize their classroom environment to elicit varied emotional responses, and who systematically observe their children, need to be sure that this information is used in constructive ways. Resource Note 6.3 provides teachers with some guidelines for using their knowledge of children's expressive styles.

RESOURCE NOTE 6.2 Identifying Children's Expressive Styles: Sample Items from Assessment Tools

Recently, researchers have developed some useful ways to observe and identify differences in how children express and regulate their feelings. Below are sample items from several of these measures; to obtain more information about these and other tools, see Appendix D.

Emotion Regulation Checklist (*Shields & Cicchetti, 1998*)

- Can modulate excitement in emotionally arousing situations
- Displays exuberance that others find intrusive or disruptive
- Displays negative emotions when attempting to engage others in play.

Hawaii Early Learning Profile (HELP) (*Parks, 1997*)

- Expresses affection
- Attempts to comfort others in distress
- Experiences difficulty with transitions

Social Competence and Behavior Evaluation (SCBE) (*LaFreniere & Dumas, 1995*)

- Comforts or assists another child in difficulty
- Accepts compromises when reasons are given
- Easily frustrated

Adjustment Scale for Preschool Intervention (*Lutz, Fantuzzo, & McDermott, 2002*)

Sample situation: How does this child cope with new learning tasks?
- Has a happy-go-lucky attitude to every problem
- Charges in without taking time to think or follow instructions
- Approaches new tasks with caution, but tries
- Won't even attempt it if he or she senses a difficulty
- Likes the challenge of something difficult
- Cannot work up the energy to face anything new

Anticipate Individual Difficulty or Enjoyment

One way that teachers can use their observations is to help them anticipate what situations may present either special difficulties or special pleasure for individual children. From her observations and notes, Hope knows that Xavier worries about new situations. She knows that Phoebe will eagerly plunge into any activity that involves pretending and creating. With this kind of knowledge, Hope can anticipate her children's likely

---

RESOURCE NOTE 6.3 Now That You Know Their Styles ... What?
Putting Knowledge of Emotions to Work

1. When planning activities, think in advance about which children may have negative or positive emotional reactions—be in tune; adapt activities to accommodate these reactions.

2. Design the program and individualize activities to fit children's differing expressive styles, as individuals and as members of distinct cultures.

3. Honor children's emotional individuality while guiding children toward using their individuality or cultural identity in ways that allow the group to function well.

---

responses to the activities she has planned, although fortunately children always have a few surprises in store.

Individualize to Fit Children's Emotional Styles

Knowing about the special characteristics of children's emotional responses and patterns of emotion communication, early childhood teachers can modify their program to build on individual children's preferences and strengths. For example, Hope has many highly expressive children in her class, who display their feelings quickly, intensely, and (usually) with much positive emotion. Her program meets their needs through a rich array of activities that allow children to express their feelings immediately and vividly. Children talk about their opinions, they draw pictures, they engage in lively debate over whether the tiger in the poem was happy or angry, whether he should be let out of his "cold cage," and how it might feel to be a tiger locked in a cage. Hope encourages this lively emotional climate but keeps it on track through clear ground rules for discussions and through well-planned transitions from one activity to the next. And because the program allows time for individual work as well as whole- and small-group activities, those children who have a lower key style feel comfortable in the classroom. Shy or reticent children also benefit from Hope's guidance and, at times, her helpful control of their explorations (Rubin, Cheah, & Fox, 2001).

Honor Children's Individuality

An emotion-centered program respects and honors individual differences. Hope refers to children's emotional states in a respectful way: "Phoebe, you're sitting there looking serious. What kind of ideas do you have?" To lively, impulsive Leo she says, "Can you wait for that until we read the poem as a group?"—acknowledging his eagerness while steering him toward postponing his outburst of excitement. Wendy closes her notebook after starting to draw her tiger picture. Hope notices this, moves closer, and says quietly, "Are you not feeling too good about that picture, Wendy?" When Serena stumbles over her words in her eagerness to explain her ideas about the tiger poem, Hope says, "Just a minute, Serena. Try to tell me again; I want to be sure I understand your idea." Watching Hope with her primary-grade class, it is clear that she delights in their individuality.

There is no limit to the ways that emotion-centered teachers can honor children's individual expressive styles. The notebooks that Hope's children keep have certain standard contents, but each is given a unique stamp by its owner. The walls of Hope's classroom are covered with children's artwork and writing. Unlike classrooms in which each piece of artwork seems produced from the same factory, these products reflect the distinctive characteristics of each child in the class. Other teachers may display close-up photographs of each child engaged in a favorite activity, showing Linda's serious attention, David's happy grin, and Latoya's astonished gaze.

OBSTACLES TO RESPECT FOR OTHERS' EMOTION EXPRESSIONS

All of us are products of our individual and cultural histories. Although at times these histories prompt our empathy and support for children's patterns of expressive behavior, at other times they create obstacles to understanding and respect.

Most of us feel more comfortable with those who share our ways. Early childhood teachers who express their feelings openly, quickly, and directly may be drawn to those children who do the same thing, and may view less expressive "deadpan" children more negatively. In contrast, adults whose own style is to keep some emotional distance and to hide both positive and negative emotions may feel uncomfortable with those children whose expressive style is very intense and direct.

Cultural patterns play a significant part in these feelings. As we have seen in earlier chapters, there are strong cultural differences in expressive behavior. Many writers have noted that African and African American groups tend to value a high level of emotional expressiveness and physical contact, while European Americans and many Asian cultures may not (Kitayama & Markus, 1994; Lynch & Hansen, 1998). Like Serena, children raised in Puerto Rican or other Latino cultures may be socialized to restrain some of their emotional expressiveness to conform to cultural standards of proper behavior toward adults (Miller & Harwood, 2001). When teachers are from different cultural groups than the children they teach, they need to work harder to develop genuine respect for children's expressive styles. The resources described in Exploration 3 in Part II will add depth to teachers' understanding of these complex cultural issues.

CONCLUSION

Respect for children's individual emotional qualities is essential to an emotion-centered early childhood program. However, respect does not necessarily imply approval or encouragement. Every early childhood teacher can think of children whose emotional responses create difficulty and unhappiness for the child and for others. Hope may respect Federico's shyness and uncertainty in new learning situations, but she may also see that Federico would benefit from increased confidence in his own abilities. Likewise, Hope may respect Nathaniel's impassioned defense of his rights, but she may urgently need to help him resolve playground disputes in better ways than wrestling children to the ground.

There's a poster that says, "I am the only me I can be right now." The purpose of this chapter has been to help early childhood professionals describe and respect that "me," as seen in each child's unique pattern of emotional responsiveness and emotion communication. The "me" displayed by Leo, Azra, Serena, Phoebe, Federico, and other young children is the unique manifestation of their genetic, familial, cultural, developmental, and social context. It represents each child's best attempt to cope with the challenges of his or her life "right now," with the tools that he or she has available.

In Chapter 7 we will return to Christine's kindergarten classroom. There we will see how early childhood teachers can create emotionally and intellectually positive learning communities, continuing to respect the "me" within each child while guiding children along satisfying, educationally valuable pathways.

Uniting Children's Learning
with Positive Emotions

Half a dozen of Christine's kindergartners are settled on the rug
looking at books and magazines that they have selected from a
nearby display shelf. Several children are lying on their stomachs,
heads propped on their hands. Others are flopped in beanbag
chairs. Matt and Ricky huddle side by side, shoulders touching,
paging through magazines. Voices rise and fall as children share

their books with each other and as they call out to children working in other parts of the room. "Martina! Martina!" Sean laughs excitedly and waves a book in the air. "I found your name!"

As she crosses the room, Christine pauses beside Matt and Ricky. She bends down. "Oh, Matt, you have my magazine about the Mayan people." Christine watches companionably as Matt continues to leaf slowly through the magazine. "If you turn the page, I think there's a picture of one of their gods." Matt turns the page, nodding with recognition as he finds the picture. "Remember when we saw a picture of where they went swimming?" Christine comments. Matt smiles broadly and nods again. Christine joins a group of children at another table. Matt turns to Ricky and tugs at Ricky's arm. He shoves the picture under Ricky's nose, pointing urgently. "Awesome!" exclaims Ricky, his eyes widening in amazement.

Christine's kindergarten classroom embodies the emotion-centered teacher's emphasis on linking positive emotions to children's learning. In this chapter, we will reflect on the way that feelings of interest and joy can motivate, sustain, and enhance children's intellectual development. Conversely, we will note that anxiety and fear may undermine learning and diminish young children's usually positive feelings about school. The chapter will describe the kinds of experiences that are most likely to produce interest and joy. It will illustrate some of the many ways that early childhood professionals can support and extend children's interests. Finally, we will see how active teacher intervention can remove roadblocks to interest development and set children on the path to new, challenging intellectual experiences.

EMOTIONS AND EARLY LEARNING

This chapter goes beyond the simplistic belief that "learning should be fun." Teachers who place a thoughtful focus on emotions select appropriate, educationally worthwhile experiences and use them to generate positive feelings in children, who are indeed "eager to learn" (Bowman, Donovan, & Burns, 2001). Furthermore, emotion-centered teachers like Christine do not manipulate children into a state of superficial excitement, which can actually interfere with learning. Rather, they try to build patterns of sustained interest and effort, while giving children opportunities to experience the joy of mastery.

Interest and Intellectual Development

Many theorists believe that specific emotions motivate specific kinds of adaptive behavior. Exploration 1 in Part II gives additional information about these theories. *Interest* has been identified as the primary emotion that motivates exploration and problem solving (Izard, 1991; Renninger et al., 1992). At first, it may be hard to think of "interest" as a strongly motivating emotion. It is easier to see how anger motivates resistance, or fear motivates escape. However, we can all think of times when feelings of curiosity have kept us working at tasks even when we are tired, hungry, or discouraged. When we are interested, we feel alert and focused; we want to explore and learn more about the object of our fascination. Feelings of curiosity make us ready to tackle a problem or pursue a question until we reach a satisfactory conclusion (Izard, 1991).

Interest enhances memory, comprehension, and selective attention (Renninger, 2000; Renninger et al., 1992). Interest is also a component of, and a sign of, *engagement*, the kind of focused involvement in tasks that has such great benefits for young children, including children with disabilities (Raspa, McWilliam, & Ridley, 2001). For all these reasons the emotion of interest plays a key role in children's intellectual development.

The Effects and Sources of Joy

Like interest, joy and happiness also foster learning and development. People are more empathic, more generous, and more creative when they are feeling joyful. Feelings of joy are accompanied by confidence, vigor, and self-esteem. Joy opens our minds and hearts to new experiences, making our mental processes more creative and flexible. When people feel joyful, they are motivated to share their thoughts and feelings with others (Izard, 1991). Toddlers and preschoolers often engage in "affective sharing," joyfully showing their special treasures to parents and teachers (Kochanska & Murray, 2000). In Christine's kindergarten, Matt happily shows his friend Ricky the "awesome" picture, and Sean shares his discovery with Martina.

Play is one of the most reliable sources of joy for young children. In fact, play researchers depend on children's expressions of happiness (smiling, laughter) to help them decide whether children's activities are playful or not. One of the reasons that children "learn through play" may be that play generally occurs in such a positive emotional climate, fostering attention, memory, and creative problem solving. Like many emotion-centered teachers, Christine organizes her program around rich opportunities for many kinds of play, including pretend play, manipulative play, and games with rules.

Mastery of some kind of challenge often brings joy in its wake. Children who have experienced the deep happiness that results from mastering a difficult skill or reaching an important goal will seek out experiences that will produce that feeling again. Sean, the child in Christine's class who found his friend Martina's name in a book, reacted to his discovery with smiles and laughter. These joyful feelings, experienced as a result of effort, will help to motivate Sean to tackle other challenges in figuring out the printed word.

Negative Emotions and Children's Learning

Just as positive emotions support learning, negative emotions can interfere with and even permanently disrupt normal intellectual development. Children who seldom experience feelings of interest may fail to develop essential competencies because they lack the emotional foundations of exploration and practice (Case, Hayward, Lewis, & Hurst, 1988; Renninger, 2000). Children who must complete academic tasks because of fear of punishment or fear of failure may complete the tasks because they want to avoid embarrassment or punishment. However, they are likely to avoid similar tasks in the future, or they may go through the motions of completing the tasks while avoiding genuine engagement.

We know from experience that feelings of anxiety limit our ability to focus attention and recall information. The level of cognitive development that children attain is partly influenced by the sheer amount of time they are able to devote to what Case calls "epistemic activities"—exploration, imitation, and problem solving (Case et al., 1988). Negative emotions such as anxiety may sharply reduce children's investment in these kinds of intelligence-building activities.

Emotions and Reactions to School

Positive emotions about learning are crucially important if children are to benefit from educational programs. We know that most children begin school with positive feelings; yet even upon entry into kindergarten, children differ in their enthusiasm, persistence, and curiosity (National Center for Education Statistics [NCES], 2002). These differences have been very powerful predictors not only of later "approaches to learning" but also of academic outcomes in first grade. Indeed, those children with positive approaches to learning were more than twice as likely as other children to score in the top 25 percent in reading and mathematics at the end of kindergarten and in first grade (NCES, 2002).

Even children who start school with positive attitudes generally feel less positive about their abilities and their school experiences with every year they spend in school. This decline is not inevitable, however. In one study, children whose preschools and parents provided them with child-focused, developmentally appropriate experiences had more positive attitudes toward school at the end of kindergarten than children whose families and preschools were more adult-directed and, at times, pressured (Hirsh-Pasek, Hyson, & Rescorla, 1990). Early childhood programs can build long-term dispositions to engage in challenging learning activities, to derive pleasure from mastering intellectual tasks, and to share knowledge and skill with others. Resource Note 7.1 provides examples of how positive emotional context may be woven into the academic expectations expressed in state standards.

RESOURCE NOTE 7.1 Breathing Emotions into Standards

Many states and national groups have adopted new standards or expected learning outcomes for young children. Some standards specifically include emotional or social outcomes, but others are focused on areas such as literacy, mathematics, and science. Even those standards can be addressed in ways that enhance their emotional relevance, thereby making learning more effective and multiplying the benefits for children. The following are some examples, using actual state standards.

THE STANDARD. "Educational experiences will assure that preschool children will recognize simple patterns and duplicate or extend them" (State of Connecticut, 1999).

Enhancing the emotional relevance. Use picture cards of facial expressions displaying different emotions to create a patterning activity—happy/sad/happy/sad/happy . . .—and invite children to extend and vary the pattern.

THE STANDARD. "Educational experiences will assure that preschool children will make and verify predictions about what will occur" (State of Connecticut, 1999).

Enhancing the emotional relevance. When designing activities to promote children's ability to make predictions, intentionally choose events that are emotionally engaging—what will happen if we build an *even higher* tower with these blocks? Will it teeter? Stay up? Crash?

THE STANDARD. "Scientific processes . . . The student asks questions about organisms, objects, and events" (Texas Education Agency, 1998).

Enhancing the emotional relevance. Create small, secure groups in which teachers and children can look at fascinating objects in "shared focus." Model your genuine interest and engagement.

THE STANDARD. "Children will develop an awareness of simple time concepts" (Georgia Office of School Readiness, 2001).

Enhancing the emotional relevance. Talk about "days to wait," and create simple calendars for emotionally meaningful events, such as birthdays, a special class party, and so on.

THE STANDARD. "Begin to demonstrate reading-like behaviors, such as pretending to read and write" (California Department of Education, 2001).

Enhancing the emotional relevance. Model your adult enjoyment and satisfaction with reading and writing in everyday activities.

THE STANDARD. "Repeats rhymes, simple songs, poems, and finger plays" (Missouri Department of Elementary and Secondary Education, 2002).

Enhancing the emotional relevance. Invite families and children to share songs and rhymes from their culture and community.

ENGAGING CHILDREN'S POSITIVE EMOTIONS: CRITICAL FEATURES

What learning activities and experiences will engage young children's interest and joy? Christine's classroom makes good use of a number of research-based techniques to strengthen children's positive dispositions about learning.

Change

"Change" gets people interested, as shown in numerous studies of attention from infancy through adulthood. Christine's classroom offers children change, but within a familiar framework. As children enter the room each day, they look around for "what's new," curious about what may be awaiting them in the room's well-defined interest areas. Before the daily free-choice time begins, Christine describes the activities that are available.

Often, small variations will rekindle children's curiosity. For example, all this week the dramatic play area has been the site for a take-out restaurant where children write down orders, make pizzas, and deliver them. Today Christine has added some carbon paper and new order pads to the area, extending interest in the dramatic play. Graphs have occupied the attention of many children over the past weeks; today Christine tells the children that they will be making a new kind of graph, to let Mrs. Madison, the school cook, know how many children want to have marshmallows in their hot chocolate. The wall above the chalkboard is already covered with graphs of many kinds. The graphs are the result of children's representations of personally meaningful information. Each one is different, and each one is the product of sustained attention and effort. One graph proclaims "MY FEMLES FAVRT FRUTS," with pictures of fruits drawn above the names of family members. Other graphs are equally personal and varied.

By spring of the kindergarten year, Christine occasionally injects larger variations into the class routine. This week, for example, was spontaneously designated as "Science Week." The week before, a child happened to bring a book of science experiments to school. Many children became fascinated with trying out these experiments, and this informal interest grew into an official "Science Week," featuring numerous science activities available during free-choice time.

In an emotion-focused early childhood program, interest-producing change is initiated both by the adults and by the children. Although this chapter's focus is on adult contributions, in a high-quality program children frequently initiate activities, vary the way activities are done, and continually contribute ideas to the life of the program.

Movement

Moving displays are inherently fascinating to children. The emotion-centered teacher does not have to become Walt Disney to tap into this source of interest, however. Christine engages children's interest with many movement-related activities and materials. The classroom aquarium, often dotted with signs directing children's attention to interesting sights, is a continual source of motion.

Every Thursday Christine and her staff perform skits dramatizing classroom issues in a visually compelling way. On this day, two student teachers presented a brief, humorous skit about a current problem, namely, that although some children have been working hard at cleaning up, others have not. The adults' vivid pantomime, as they stacked blocks, gestured indignantly, and stomped out of the room, fully engaged the children's interest and stimulated lively discussion of possible fair solutions.

Besides watching others' movements, Christine's kindergartners are intensely interested in producing movement of their own. Whether making and swinging a sand pendulum, dressing up in seasonal clothing and prancing down a fashion runway, or observing and recording the speed at which objects hit the floor when dropped from a height, movement-related activities capture the sustained attention of the class.

Faces

While intense interest in the human face peaks in infancy, faces—and the relationships they represent—remain sources of pleasure and curiosity in later years. Christine uses this interest effectively, getting down close to children and communicating with children through her own facial expressions. This interest in faces may also account for the children's fascination with some new computer software that displays photographs of the children in the class. On this morning, Lily, Anna, and Pauline spent 15 minutes intensely focused on the computer, identifying the children in the pictures and manipulating various features of the program.

Mastery

Opportunities for mastery—especially if the task is moderately challenging and includes supportive adult feedback—bring forth interest, joy, and pride in infants and young children (Kelly, Brownell, & Campbell, 2000; Redding, Morgan, & Harmon, 1988). It is difficult to know where to begin in describing the many opportunities for child control and mastery available in Christine's kindergarten class. At group time, Christine calls one child to her side and poses a "question of the day" in a gamelike format. These questions, which are a regular feature of morning meetings, are invariably related to classroom activities and encourage reflection and recall. Today the question to Danny was, "In our pizza shop, can you name three kinds of toppings available to our customers?" (Whispered hints from Christine are sometimes needed, and the rest of the children have no objection, since the point is success, not competition. At times, a group of children will work together to arrive at the answer, bringing special delight to those children whose cultures emphasize collective rather than individual accomplishment.) When Danny—with no hints—comes up with pepperoni, cheese, and mushrooms, the class cheers and Danny grins delightedly at his mastery of the day's question.

Mastery opportunities during group time form only a small part of Christine's curriculum. Throughout the day, the children select many of their own activities from choices provided by the teacher. Within these activities, there are many ways for children to be "in charge." In the pizza shop, for example, children choose roles they will assume. They write down the customers' orders, make the pizzas with play dough and construction paper, and deliver them with a flourish. Interest and joy are evident on the faces of the children who are involved in this activity.

The day's graphing activity offered children another source of control. By stating their individual or group preferences and communicating them to the school cook, the children could influence what they received for snack. Children in Christine's class know that they can approach problems in a variety of ways. The graph Christine had set up had two columns: "Marshmallows" and "No Marshmallows." However, Aaron declared, "I don't care whether I have marshmallows or not." Christine responded, "Whoops—I should have written three columns on our graph: Marshmallows, No Marshmallows, and Don't Care. Maybe next time I will do that."

Another class discussion further illustrates how opportunities for control stimulate children's interest. Christine explained to the class that the tape recorder had broken because children were pushing the buttons incorrectly (apparently this had been discussed before with no effect). Now, Christine said, the class had no tape recorder, and the director was not sure they should buy another one right away because the same thing might happen again. In some classrooms this kind of discussion turns into a teacher-directed scolding for past mistakes. However, Christine then asked the children how they thought the director might be persuaded to buy another tape recorder. "We could promise not to hit the buttons so hard," one child suggested. "We could make a sign telling kids not to push two buttons at the same time," was another suggestion, countered with, "But I can't read." "A picture sign!" suggested yet another child. Finally the class agreed that they would all try to remember to be careful using the new tape recorder and that a large pictorial reminder would be posted in the listening area. Christine said that she would discuss the children's ideas with the director and see whether the arguments would convince her to try the tape recorder again. This whole dialogue was intensely interesting to the children, since they could see that they had the opportunity to influence the outcome of events that were important to them.

JUMP-STARTS FOR CHILDREN'S INTEREST

Emotion-centered teachers recognize that children will usually seek out activities and materials that stimulate their interest and that hold out the possibility of mastery (see Resource Note 7.2). Teachers can also be reasonably confident that, as children develop, most of them will broaden their interests and extend them into areas that are important for later academic success and full personal development.

RESOURCE NOTE 7.2 Will This Activity Engage Children's
Positive Emotions? An Emotion Checkup

Use this guide when planning activities. Most of the time it will be easy to adapt an activity to engage children's interest, increase joy, and (sometimes) produce surprise. This does *not* mean simply making activities more "fun." Emotional engagement often comes from increasing the challenge of activities, not making them easier or cuter.

Suggestions for Increasing the Emotional Value of Activities

- Create a small but interesting variation on the familiar themes or patterns that the class has relied on so far.
- Use movement—by the children or by some aspects of the activity—to heighten their interest and involvement.
- Tap into children's innate interest in faces and face-like displays, using photographs of people, the children's own faces, and those of adults who are close to them.
- Increase the ways in which children can be in control or show mastery during the activity.

Sample Activities to Modify Using these Suggestions

- A science lesson in which the teacher had planned to demonstrate how ice melts.
- An art activity using markers, glue, and paper.
- A writing center in which pens and paper are offered.
- A mathematics activity in which children are invited to compare two groups of objects to see which group has more.
- A literacy activity to develop children's ability to identify letter sounds.
- Another activity you have planned or would like to do again.

Roadblocks to Interest Development

However, for many reasons children's interests may not always develop spontaneously. Children may come into the early childhood program having had little encouragement of their interests and having had few opportunities to feel the joy of mastery. Fearful of scorn or punishment, they may avoid most learning activities. Other children may be temperamentally inhibited, reluctant to try anything new (Henderson & Fox, 1998). Some children's family environment or culture may discourage attempts at mastery or may emphasize group rather than individual success. Children living in Native American, Latino, or Asian cultures may hesitate to try anything that will force them to compete or set them above other children. These cultural standards should be respected. Thoughtful teachers will recognize and effectively address the challenges posed by these standards, when children enter educational settings that are based on European American norms of individual achievement (Lynch & Hanson, 1998).

In addition to these individual variations (also discussed in Exploration 3 in Part II), teachers may also find that children do not always "naturally" gravitate toward the skills that our culture requires them to master. Curriculum is defined by sociocultural values (what the culture and society deem worth knowing) as well as by children's spontaneous interests and needs (Rogoff & Morelli, 1989; Spodek & Saracho, 1996). This issue becomes particularly pressing by first and second grade, when our society expects children to master basic literacy and mathematical concepts and to begin to acquire conventional knowledge of historical events and places. Although children seem intrinsically motivated to master many of these skills, the process is not always seamless or painless.

Teachers' "Interest Interventions": Falling Objects

For all these reasons, emotion-centered teachers frequently intervene to take children beyond what may naturally interest them. A spontaneous science activity that Christine organized highlights some of these techniques.

> Christine began the activity by calling the group together on the rug. "This is another one of the experiments from Martina's book," Christine explained. "This one is a *lot* of fun; I think you may really like it. It's a "Falling Objects" experiment, and we'll try it out first with everyone here. If you don't get a chance to do it right now, you can try it during free-choice time."
>
> The children scooched closer on the carpet. "Now," said Christine, "we are going to need someone to be the Recorder." Juliette waved her hand eagerly. "Your job, Juliette, is going to be to write down what people find out about the falling objects. Here's your recording notebook." (The children

had been recording the results of other experiments earlier in the week and liked the job of Recorder very much.) Next, Christine had two children volunteer to be the Scientific Observers of the falling objects. In hard hats, the two Observers lay on the floor. Above them, Quentin stood on a table. He selected two objects from a basket and held them up.

"What we have to do," Christine declared, "is to figure out which object will hit the ground first." Quentin held up a whiffle ball and a soccer ball. "Which one do you think will hit the ground first?" Christine asked the group in an interested tone. "I think the whiffle ball," said Tracy. "Why do you think that?" asked Christine, again in a sincerely curious tone of voice. "Well," reflected Tracy, "the whiffle ball has air in it, and the soccer ball doesn't." "But the soccer ball is heavier," Matt interrupted. "Heavier things go faster." "No they *don't*, Matt," Sean patiently explained. "I think Matt's right," Ricky said loyally. "The soccer ball *should* go faster. But I don't know if it *will*."

"Let's see," said Christine. "Quentin can drop the balls at the same time and the observers can watch to see which one hits the ground first. How many times should we try it?" The class agreed on three tries. Everyone watched intently as the balls were dropped, cheering if their favorite was the winner. Juliette recorded the results in her notebook, deciding to use *F* for *Faster* under a picture of the balls Quentin was dropping.

This activity is described in detail, not because it is necessarily a model for teaching a scientific concept, but as an example of how teachers can intervene to broaden the sources of interest and joy for young children. Many aspects of Christine's guidance of this activity contributed to its emotion-engaging power.

Christine's own affective engagement in scientific pursuits invests the activity with significance for children. As we saw in an earlier chapter, Christine spontaneously models the kinds of emotional responses she hopes children will develop in their kindergarten learning. Her enthusiasm for this activity and her curiosity about the outcome do not seem contrived. Teachers sometimes fake curiosity: "Goodness, boys and girls, I *wonder* what will happen when we put a brick into the tub of water. Will it sink or will it float? I just can't wait to see!" Such contrived interest is fundamentally disrespectful, and perceptive children see right through it. In contrast, Christine's involvement in this activity, and in other science activities throughout the year, is spontaneous and genuine. And because the children are emotionally attached to Christine (Hamre & Pianta, 2001; Howes & Ritchie, 2002), they are more likely to become interested in activities and skills that Christine values.

Christine has definite goals for this and other science activities. Certainly, she has the science content standards in mind. But a major goal is to help the children view themselves as scientists, capable of engaging in scientific work. Children's feelings of control and mastery are highlighted by this activity. Children—both boys and girls—get to enact scientific roles, observing, recording, making, and verifying predictions. Yet they can choose what roles they prefer to play, including just watching for a while if they prefer. Juliette's earlier interest in writing and in making little books is now being applied in a new domain. Matt and Ricky's friendship and love of pretend play are extended to a new role—being the hard-hatted observers for the experiment.

Christine plays a very active role in this first go-around of the Falling Objects experiment. Without controlling every aspect of the activity, she guides the class through the activity, posing questions, encouraging children to explain their predictions, highlighting features of the objects being dropped, reminding children of their jobs in the experiment. ("Did you remember to write down which was faster that time, Juliette? We can put the book on our science shelf later.") At the conclusion of the whole-class portion of the experiment, Christine invites the children to try the activity during free-choice time and organizes another group of children to start it off. From time to time, Christine checks back with the children to see how they are using the materials.

This description shows how emotion-centered teachers can extend the range of educationally worthwhile experiences that give children satisfaction and pleasure. Christine links these new experiences in scientific experimentation with earlier emotionally positive experiences. In the science experiment and in casual conversation with children, Christine frequently makes reference to children's previous successes and their enjoyment of other, similar activities. "Remember when we saw the picture of them swimming?" she commented to Matt as he attempted to read the magazine. Matt's smile showed that this was an emotionally positive memory for him. The math graphs on the wall had to do with pleasurable topics of personal relevance for children; for example, their family's favorite foods, their own hair color, and their cookie preferences.

EXTENDING CHILDREN'S INTERESTS

Besides jump-starting children's interest in new intellectual pursuits through active interventions, Christine and other early childhood professionals have numerous other ways to extend children's engagement in learning.

Honoring Preferences

As children get older they increasingly develop individual or collective activity preferences. Although these preferences—which occasionally become brief obsessions—may restrict children's willingness to try new experiences, those same preferences also may be used as bridges from the familiar to the new. One of the strengths of the project approach to curriculum (Helm & Katz, 2001; Katz & Chard, 2000) is that children may participate in a class project in a variety of ways. Christine's Science Week activities were designed to appeal to the interests of children who "specialize" in drawing, writing, ball playing, and so on. The emphasis on small-group, cooperative investigations allowed children to move into a new area of learning within a framework of comfortable, preferred activities.

Providing Time

Christine's program provides children with enough time to explore new learning experiences, thus extending children's emotional range. When confronted with an unfamiliar material or experience, most children go through a predictable sequence. They may hang back for a bit, and then they begin to explore in a random sort of way. After a time of "aimless" exploration, children may shift intellectual gears and become deeply focused on serious systematic investigations, followed by more playful, creative variations. This kind of sequence (Bredekamp & Rosegrant, 1992) is likely to lead to feelings of mastery and to the development of positive dispositions to encounter new experiences. However, the sequence can be short-circuited when early childhood teachers rush children from one "exciting" new activity to another. In her science experiment, Christine went beyond a one-shot, teacher-led demonstration. Rather, she engaged the entire group in an initial exploration and guided children to return to the activity throughout the day and beyond.

Other activities in Christine's room also encourage this sequence of exploration and systematic investigation. The writing center is always available for children to draw, scribble, copy, and compose letters or stories. Free exploration is balanced with times when Christine prompts children to attempt specific writing tasks.

Conveying Confidence

Children's positive emotional responses to learning are broadened when the teacher believes that children are capable of tackling new and possibly difficult material. "High expectations" can receive a bad name because some early childhood educators believe that children should not have too much pressure put on them. However, there is a difference between expectations that are pressuring and an emotionally supportive belief that children are capable of doing great things. "You can be good observers," Christine comments to Matt and Ricky, the first two volunteers. "You have good eyes, and you notice a lot of things." "Juliette, you are a good recorder because you like to write things down." Sometimes Christine will refer to children that she taught at another school, saying, "I don't know if you guys can do this. My children in New York had a really hard time with it." A loud chorus of "We can do it!" usually follows this. On the printed page, these words may suggest an overemphasis on competition. However, as spoken in Christine's classroom, they sound a different note. Through these kinds of playful challenges, Christine conveys to her children that she admires them, that she thinks it is interesting and fun to try hard activities, and that it is okay to try something and have it not work out.

Scaffolding and Support

Christine and other emotion-centered teachers also recognize that certain children may require a higher degree of teacher scaffolding if they are to come out of a challenging experience with positive feelings. This may mean holding a young child on one's lap while the child tries a difficult puzzle. Hesitant older children may require physical closeness and a tactful hint now and then. Young children with disabilities often need their teachers to intervene more actively than children without disabilities (Bredekamp & Copple, 1997; Sandall, McLean, & Smith, 2000). However, children without disabilities may also enter the early childhood program lacking confidence in their own skills. For all these children, the emotion-centered teacher must achieve a thoughtful balance between two extremes: just waiting for the children to try new activities on their own, and rushing the children into challenges that may create anxiety and undermine their positive learning dispositions.

The options available for teachers to build on children's interests are limitless. Resource Note 7.3 offers a summary of some of the options outlined in this chapter. All can be readily adapted to children's individual and cultural characteristics and to the setting in which you teach.

CONCLUSION

In *Bread and Jam for Frances* (Hoban, 1964), the little badger's parents yield to her food fussiness and give her a steady diet of her favorite, bread and jam. As time goes by, what Frances had longed for becomes dull and unappetizing. When Frances finally asks for some of the family's spaghetti and meatballs, her parents "naively" comment that they thought Frances did not like spaghetti. Frances's lament—"How do you know what I'll like if you won't even try me?"—captures children's need for the teacher-activist approach described in this chapter.

Teachers of young children need to do more than give children a sweet, steady, intellectually shallow diet of things they already like. Being offered new experiences—and being supported in trying them out—pro-

RESOURCE NOTE 7.3 Making Positive Emotion Links
by Extending Children's Interests

Starting where children already are, teachers can extend children's interest and engagement in learning in the following ways:

- Honor children's preferences for certain kinds of activities.
   Extend projects to offer many ways to incorporate individual preferences.
   Build in attention to preferences through a daily schedule that offers child choice and small group activities.
   Respect individual and cultural preferences, making sure activities support collaborative or group efforts as well as individual accomplishments.
- Provide time for extended investigations and exploration of new learning experiences.
   Respect the sometimes lengthy cycle of free exploration and focused investigation, which decreases fear of new challenges and allows deep involvement.
   Get involved at key times to prompt and challenge children to take the experience one step further.
- Convey confidence that children can tackle difficult learning challenges successfully.
   Create high expectations in an encouraging climate.
   Show that you know children can learn and succeed—and enjoy the challenge.
- Give extra scaffolding and support to children who need extra help to engage successfully in new or challenging learning experiences.
   Recognize difference in children's need for scaffolding if they are to become confident learners.
   Pay special attention to the needs of children with disabilities and children who have experienced obstacles to successful learning.

vides children with a chance to develop new likes, new enthusiasms, and new areas of competence. Teachers sometimes hesitate to be too activist out of fear of pushing children. Although this fear is well founded, the other extreme is also risky. Some children automatically assume that they will hate any new experience. Sometimes this declaration covers their fears that they will fail or look silly. Some children may be temperamentally inhibited and simply need a longer period of familiarization.

In broadening children's intellectual diet, teachers can help by expressing confidence that children could have a different feeling about things later on. "When I was a little girl, I remember that I didn't want to go to the gym. I thought I might fall when I had to climb the rope. But my teacher held me and I practiced and finally I learned to climb up the rope." Sometimes it is appropriate to require that children "taste" new experiences—not just once, but repeatedly—to give them a chance to explore and investigate. A great advantage of mixed-age groups, such as the one in Hope's primary class, is that children can observe and work side by side with older, more skilled children—but still children close in age—who are taking on new educational challenges and experiencing interest, pride, and joy in their efforts.

The conclusion of this chapter brings us full circle in our investigation of all aspects of an emotion-centered curriculum. None of Christine's efforts to create curious, joyful learners would be possible without an emotion-centered philosophy of education, firmly grounded in theory and the wisdom of practice. As they investigate Mayan gods and falling whiffle balls, the secure emotional environment Christine has created supports the children. They work well together because they are gaining understanding of how they and others feel, in part through Christine's modeling of authentic, appropriate emotions. They are able to sustain their engagement in these challenging activities because of their growing competence at emotion regulation. And each of Christine's children feels that his or her unique emotional style, and the style of his or her culture, is a valued part of the class. Like the children who experience the loving care and education given by Natalie, Hope, Terry, Denise, and all emotion-focused early childhood professionals, these children thrive because feelings are at the very center of their early childhood program.

PART II

Going Deeper: Exploring Emotions and Their Development

This part of *The Emotional Development of Young Children* gives you the opportunity to explore more deeply the history, theoretical perspectives, and research surrounding the rich topic of early emotional development. Each exploration is organized around a vignette, featuring two additional emotion-centered practitioners: Ilene, a Head Start teacher, and Leslie, a family child care provider. Each vignette is followed by a set of reflections and questions that encourage you to apply your understanding of young children's emotions to the scenes described. To help you do this, material from earlier chapters is supplemented with concise summaries of key information, along with recommended readings from some of the many recent publications on early emotional development, emotional competence, and early intervention.

The first exploration invites you to examine in detail the way that various theories have defined the place of emotions in development and learning. The second exploration uses the same approach to explore the stages and sequences in which children come to express, understand, and regulate emotions. The final exploration takes up the question of how biology, the environment, and a variety of individual differences may affect how children develop emotionally.

Anger, Interest, Fear, and Joy: What Are Emotions For?

The 4-year-olds in Ilene's Head Start class are winding up a long indoor free-play period. Soft music plays in the background. Alone in the block area, Phillip lies on the floor, his body relaxed, slowly pushing a wooden crane back and forth on the rug. From time to time he stops, rolls onto his back, and gazes idly at the ceiling. Then he returns to manipulating the crane. Phillip's tongue sticks out to one side as he untangles the string that hooks objects to the crane. Will approaches from across the room. As he gets closer to Phillip, he peeks shyly at what Phillip is doing from under his lowered brows and then quickly looks away. Will picks up a bulldozer from the shelf and seats himself on the rug a few feet from Phillip. He begins to push his bulldozer back and forth, mirroring Phillip's actions but not looking at him.

Across the room four children sit on chairs, dangling fishing poles into a container of toy fish. Shrieks of delight are heard as they catch fish with the magnets on the end of their fishing poles. The children bounce up and down on their chairs in excitement and clap at their own success. As fish are caught, the children quickly pull them off the magnet hooks and toss them back in the "pond" for another try.

Hannah is exploring an indoor climbing apparatus set up in a secluded corner. With the children's help, the apparatus had been constructed to resemble a beehive (a class project about bees had been underway for a week, stimulated in part by the appearance of bees on the playground). Ilene, the head teacher, places a reassuring hand on Hannah's back as Hannah warily ascends the climber's ladder and emerges high atop the platform. Slowly, her fearful expression changes to a delighted smile as she surveys the room from her new vantage point. Min joins Hannah. The two girls, both wearing pipe cleaner antennae, play "bees," making the circuit of the beehive over and over, grinning at one another every time they reach the platform. Hannah buzzes loudly, grimaces, and jabs a pointed finger at a nearby adult as she rounds the corner for another trip to the hive. "Sting, sting, sting," she chants triumphantly.

The noise level in the room rises. Children's voices weave and overlap—loud, hesitant, whining, confident, amazed, outraged: "Ilene! Ilene! Look at mine!" "Look at this one!" "Wait a minute— I didn't get a turn." "You're pushing me off—stop it, Ben!" "Can I have a piece of that?" "Watch out! Here it comes!"

Tiny, intense Charlene begins to bustle from one group to another, shouting officiously, "It's cleanup time! Cleanup time!" as she glares at children who are still playing. Her message to the block builders is met with Daniel's even louder response: "SHUT UP! I KNOW THAT!" Charlene tosses her head, curls her lip disdainfully, and stomps away to another group.

As children finish cleaning up, they gather on the rug to look at books. Daniel scans the selections on the book display shelf. His eyes widen as he sees a book he especially likes. Pulling it off the shelf, Daniel holds his choice above his head, smiling joyously as he heads for his favorite parent helper's lap and snuggles close to her.

As these 4-year-olds worked and played, there was never a moment when emotions were absent. And whether by supporting, discouraging, or ignoring children's emotions, adults are drawn into the children's emotional lives. This exploration invites you to consider the nature and purpose of emotions while examining traditional as well as new perspectives on early emotional development.

1. *Emotions and their expression.* What emotions are the children in Ilene's group expressing? How are they expressing them? If you are working with young children, consider the similarities and differences between the description in the vignette above and your own class.

2. *Adult responses.* Adults might respond in many different ways to these emotions. What are some examples of possible responses? Which responses would you favor, and why?

3. *Developmental and learning theories.* Just as teachers and other adults have different ideas about the value and purpose of children's emotions, so do different theories of child development. Each has a distinctive perspective, and each contributes to our insight into children's emotional development. You may begin to explore these differing perspectives with the few examples below. The readings recommended at the end of this exploration provide deeper and more comprehensive insights.

- Freud's theory emphasizes that children have powerful angry feelings, which are often acted out symbolically. From this perspective, what might be the meaning of Hannah "stinging" her teacher?
- Erik Erikson's theory is similar to Freud's in some respects but places great emphasis on children's desire to master scary or confusing experiences, often through play. Do you see this mastery motivation in Hannah's emotional expressions when she is on the climber?
- Erikson also describes specific stages of development, each with its own emotion-related conflict. For 4-year-olds, this conflict is between *initiative*—the drive to be powerful and in charge—and *guilt*—the sense of danger or risk that this initiative may bring. Are there examples of this conflict in the vignette? In the children with whom you work?
- Piaget's theory of development focuses on cognition, but he also believed that emotions provide the "energy" for cognitive development. Where in the vignette and in the children you know can you see the motivational power of emotions?
- Learning theories emphasize the contributions of the environment to individual children's emotional responses. As you reread the vignette, consider what early experiences in children's family or community environments might have shaped their current emotion-related behavior.

- Vygotsky's theory reflects a social constructivist perspective on development, including children's emotional development. Other people—adults or somewhat more skilled peers—"scaffold" and promote children's use of ever more advanced skills. Social pretend play creates many opportunities for children to experience and express complex emotions, at a higher level than they might on their own. Again, where do you see examples?

4. *Adequacy of developmental theories for understanding emotions.* Thinking about several theories of child development, which one seems to you to have the most to offer in understanding the emotional aspects of the scene in Ilene's Head Start classroom? Is one theory adequate, or are you more comfortable combining elements from several? And finally, are there things that all these theories leave out?

5. *New perspectives on emotional development.* Although these theories can help explain aspects of young children's emotions, none was specifically developed to focus on emotions, and none produced much research on early emotional development. But from the 1980s on, new perspectives on emotions have influenced theory and research. The "new emotions researchers" don't agree on everything, but they share three key ideas: (a) Emotions help humans survive and adapt; (b) emotions guide and motivate behavior; and (c) emotions support communication with others.

- *Survival and adaptation.* If emotions are essential to human survival and adaptation, they must have universal characteristics. What do you see in the expressions or behavior of the children in Ilene's class that you would see anywhere, any time, in any culture? In contrast, what expressions or behavior seem specific to certain children or environments?
- *Motivation.* If emotions are the underlying motivation for human behavior, how do you see this connection in the vignette? How did Daniel's feelings of anger influence his behavior? And what emotions might have influenced Will to behave the way he did? Even though anger may have evolved to help human beings overcome danger and survive, does that mean teachers should encourage Daniel to act as he did? How can we acknowledge the value of anger (think about how anger at injustice has motivated political action) while guiding children toward appropriate expressions?
- *Communication.* If emotions help human beings to communicate, what examples may be found in Ilene's class? Consider facial, vocal, verbal, and gestural communications. How do Ilene and other teachers pick up on these communicative signals? Also think about yourself as an adult: Although your signals may be less direct than Daniel's or Charlene's, how do your emotions help you communicate with others?

CONCLUSION

Emotions have important functions in human life. Each of the major theories of development and behavior has addressed this issue, but none has told a comprehensive story about the significance of emotions in children's lives.

The story of early emotional development has gained scope and power through the expansion in emotions research from the 1980s to the present. These scholars remind us that emotions are universal. They offer convincing examples that both "positive" and "negative" emotions have helped human beings to survive, adapt, and learn. They remind us that the unspoken language of feeling binds us together, transcending boundaries of culture and age.

Despite these common links, the expression, understanding, and regulation of emotions do change as children grow. Exploration 2 will use a scene from Leslie's family child care program to highlight some of these changes over the first 8 years of life.

READINGS FOR FURTHER EXPLORATION

Berk, L., & Winsler, A. (1995). *Scaffolding children's learning: Vygotsky and early childhood education.* Washington, DC: NAEYC.

> Provides an introduction to Vygotsky's theory and offers practical applications for curriculum and teaching practices.

Cicchetti, D., & Hesse, P. (1983). Affect and intellect: Piaget's contributions to the study of infant emotional development. In R. Plutchik & H. Kellerman (Eds.), *Emotion: Theory, research, and experience: Vol. 2. Emotions in early development* (pp. 115–170). New York: Academic Press.

> A thought-provoking perspective on Piaget, who is often believed to have focused only on cognitive development.

Hyson, M.C. (1996). Theory: An analysis (Part 2). In J. A. Chafel & S. Reifel (Eds.), *Advances in early education and day care: Theory and practice in early childhood teaching* (Vol. 8, pp. 41–89). Greenwich, CT: JAI Press.

> Describes the functions, influence, and limitations of various theories in relation to early childhood education. Discusses major child development theories and other theoretical perspectives.

Hyson, M. C., & Cone, J. (1989). Giving form to feeling: Emotions research and early childhood education. *Journal of Applied Developmental Psychology, 10*(3), 375–399.

> Provides detailed discussion and comparison of specific child development theories as they explain and predict young children's emotional development.

Izard, C. E. (1991). *The psychology of emotions.* New York: Plenum.

> A full discussion of emotions and emotional development by a leading theorist who emphasizes emotions' evolutionary and adaptive functions.

Miller, P. H. (2002). *Theories of developmental psychology* (4th ed.) New York: Worth.

> A comprehensive review and comparison of major developmental theories.

Saarni, C., Mumme, D. L., & Campos, J. J. (1998). Emotional development: Action, communication, and understanding. In N. Eisenberg (Ed.), *Handbook of child psychology: Social, emotional, and personality development: Vol. 3*, (5th ed., pp. 237–311). New York: Wiley.

> A thorough scholarly review of theories and research on children's emotional development.

Sroufe, L. A. (1996). *Emotional development: The organization of emotional life in the early years.* New York: Cambridge University Press.

> A readable description of how children's emotional competence may grow during early childhood. Links emotional development to the formation of children's attachment to significant adults.

Young Children's Emotional Development: What Can We Expect?

At 10 o'clock on a cold February morning, Leslie, a family child care provider, has settled her children in her sunny living room. Some of the children are gathered around a table on which Leslie has set out a container of play dough with rollers and cutters. Others are examining colored paper and scissors, while 8-week-old Andy, the youngest member of the group, looks on from his infant swing. His eyes follow the older children's movements and his expression brightens as children stop to look him in the eye and show him their toys. "He's our baby," 6-year-old Mary Anne tells the visitor with a proprietary air, reveling in her "special helper" status on a day off from school.

Three-and-a-half-year-old Zachary, 3-year-old Denise, and 2-year-old Caitlin work with the dough. Zachary sorts through the dough cutters looking for his favorite. "Another truck!" he exclaims, crinkling his nose in delight and waving the cutter above his head. He bends over his dough, placing his two truck cutters side by side and carefully pressing them into the play dough. Beside him, Caitlin plunges her fingers into her piece of dough, smiling with pleasure.

Abigail, who is 18 months old, approaches the play dough table. Abigail reaches across Zachary for a chunk of his dough. He sees her coming and protects his dough with his whole body. Abigail leans her sturdy shoulder against Zachary's and reaches under his arm. "Hey!" Zachary announces in a commanding tone. "No roughhousin' in here!"

Abigail whines and then squeals, looking appealingly at Leslie. She stomps her feet in a rhythmic dance of frustration as Zachary continues to protect his dough with righteous indignation. "Have something *else*," he declares, pressing his lips together. "I need my play dough." Abigail falls to the floor, sobbing and hiccupping. She stares straight ahead, lost in misery. Across the room, Mary Anne sizes up the situation and digs Abigail's blanket out of a basket. She approaches Abigail, handing her the blanket with a look of concern. Abigail stuffs her thumb in her mouth and caresses the blanket's satin binding.

During their play time in Leslie's living room, Andy, Caitlin, Zachary, Denise, Abigail, and Mary Anne displayed the full range of basic human emotions described in Exploration 1, including interest, joy, sadness, and anger. Every child smiled and laughed; every child expressed at least some anger or frustration during the morning; every child's interest was engaged by the people, materials, and activities in Leslie's program.

Despite these common characteristics, a visitor to Leslie's family child care home would be struck by age-related variations in the children's emotional responses. This vignette from Leslie's family child care home, the questions that follow, and the readings for further exploration will give greater depth to your understanding of developmental changes in children's expression, understanding, and regulation of emotions over the first 8 years of life.

1. *Age-related differences.* The children in Leslie's family child care home range in age from 8 weeks to 6 years. What are some of the most striking differences in their expression and regulation of emotions?

2. *Changes in facial expressions of emotion.* Leslie's children—and all children, as well as adults—express feelings through their faces. As they get older, one of the ways in which children change is in their ability to express emotions through smiles, frowns, and other expressions of feeling. Think about newborn babies—what expressions do you see? And then, what do you see when caring for a 6-month-old? A 1-year-old? A 2- or 3-year-old? Most of the basic emotions can be seen on children's faces from the first months of life, but are there emotions that become expressed more often at certain ages?

3. *Showing complex emotions.* Some facial expressions—those showing pride, shame, shyness, embarrassment, contempt, and guilt—are simply not seen in young babies. In this vignette, what complex emotions are expressed by the older toddlers and preschoolers in Leslie's group (Denise, Caitlin)? Consider the cognitive abilities that are needed to experience and express these feelings.

4. *Body language.* Faces do not do the whole job, at every age, children use their whole bodies to express emotions. Consider the children in this vignette—what gestures and body language are they using? What advantages do the older children have, in their ability to use their bodies to express emotions? How does this fit with your own experience with children of different ages?

5. *Sounds and words.* With age and development, children become better at expressing their feelings in sounds and words. How does Leslie—and how do you and other professionals—figure out what babies are feeling, even when they do not know words? Once children can talk, they begin to use simple labels for their feelings, and later, more complex descriptions. Again, consider the children in Leslie's group as well as children with whom you have worked.

6. *Symbolic representations.* From the toddler years through preschool and beyond, children also become better at using symbols—pretend play, drawings, manipulative materials—to communicate and master emotions. What benefits are there in being able to represent emotions symbolically? How can you promote the development of those representational abilities?

7. *Emotion knowledge.* Emotion knowledge—identifying and naming their own and others' feelings—is an essential foundation for children's regulation of emotions, for empathy, and for appropriate prosocial behavior. Children begin to understand emotions earlier than we used to think, and toddlers can label basic emotions, although complex or mixed emotions take longer to understand. From toddlerhood through preschool, children also gain insight into why people might feel the way they do, into how their own feelings might differ from others', and into their environment's spoken and unspoken expectations about when and how to show emotions. In this vignette, what clues are evident about the children's varying levels of emotion knowledge? What do the children with whom you work seem to know about emotions, and how might you assess this (see Appendix D)?

8. *Age changes in emotion regulation.* Age-related changes also take place in children's ability to control or regulate their emotional states. Chapter 5 focused on early childhood teachers' roles in helping children gain skills in emotion regulation. In this vignette, what differences do you see in the younger and older children's regulatory competence? Are there strategies that even the youngest children seem to be using? Babies' brains are not yet organized to allow them to inhibit their expression of strong feelings, but look for clues as to how older children can mask or disguise emotions, or even exaggerate them as Abigail seems to be doing. And of course older children are better able to conform to whatever unwritten rules exist in their culture and community, about showing or hiding emotions.

9. *Responses to others' feelings.* Researchers find strong evidence that even young babies are aware of others' emotional reactions. Do you see this in the vignette and in your experience? From 8 or 9 months on, children also begin to use "social referencing" to check adults' emotional reactions in uncertain situations. Again, you may find examples in the vignette. And toddlers like Abigail seem to enjoy getting others to show strong emotions; it seems to be one way they learn about feelings. Empathy also develops over time, from "preempathic behaviors" like Andy's contagious distress to more mature forms: Where do you see this? And finally, at different ages children's emotional reactions to the same situation may be quite different; for example, toddlers may show fear and older children may show fascination at the sight of a large, quickly moving dog.

10. *Emotional ties to others.* From the earliest weeks, ties of comfort and love bind children to others. Attachment to important adults grows over time, from more general or indiscriminate relationships to very specific connections with mother, father, or a special caregiver like Leslie. How may the younger and older children in the vignette differ in the ties they have to Leslie and in how they show their need for her? Emotional bonds with other children also develop over the early childhood years—more quickly in children who have spent much time in child care or with siblings. Again, how do Leslie's children and the children you teach show age-related changes in their emotional bonds with their peers?

11. *Stage models of emotional development: Greenspan, Fischer, Saarni.* Some scholars have developed comprehensive descriptions of stages or sequences of emotional development. Table 1 compares three such descriptions—those of Stanley Greenspan, Kurt Fischer, and Carolyn Saarni.

Each is grounded in a somewhat different theoretical perspective, with Greenspan's model being more psychodynamic, Fischer's more cognitively focused on the growth of specific emotion skills, and Saarni's coming out of a social constructivist perspective. Using this table and the recommended readings below, can you identify in the vignette examples of behavior that correspond to some of these theoretical perspectives? Andy's behavior, for example, might correspond to what Greenspan calls "self-

TABLE 1. Stage Models of Emotional Development

Greenspan	Fischer	Saarni
0–3 months Self-regulation and interest in the world *2–7 months* "Falling in love" *3–10 months* Developing intentional communication *9–18 months* Emergence of an organized sense of self *18–36 months* Creating emotional ideas *30–48 months* Emotional thinking—the basis for fantasy, reality, and self-esteem	*Birth–6 months* Tier 1: Reflexes: components of basic emotional reactions *6 months–18 months* Tier 2: Sensorimotor action patterns for basic emotions (as development proceeds through Tier 2, various "action clusters" become better coordinated) *18 months+* Tier 3: Representations of emotion situations through pretend play and spontaneous language (as development proceeds through Tier 3, emotion representations become more complex but continue to deal with concrete events and immediate experiences)	*0–12 months* Self-soothing Regulation of attention in service of coordinated action Reliance on caregivers to scaffold at stressful times More discrimination of others' emotion expressions Increasing coordination of expressive behavior with situations that elicit emotions. Social referencing Using emotion signals for social purposes ("fake crying") *12 months–2 ½ yrs* Self-awareness emerges Irritability when growing need for exploration is thwarted Self-evaluation and self-consciousness seen in behaviors showing shame, pride, coyness More understanding and use of emotion language Increasing understanding of what others' feelings mean Early forms of empathy and prosocial action *2 ½–5 years* Growing use of symbols to represent emotions Use of pretend emotions in dramatic play and teasing Aware of ability to mislead others by putting on false expressions By communicating with others, learns more about how to behave in social situations Sympathetic to other children; helping behavior Increasing insight into others' emotions *5–7 years* Tries to regulate own self-conscious emotions (shame, pride, embarrassment) Still needs adults for help but relies more on own coping and problem solving Adopts "cool" emotional front with peers More coordination of social skills with own and other children's feelings Begins to coordinate agreed-on "emotion scripts" with others

regulation and interest in the world." You might also consider and classify your own children's emotional development in light of the stages and sequences in this table.

12. *Putting the changes together: Themes and trends across models*. Greenspan, Fischer, and Saarni emphasize somewhat different things, but they and others agree on the big picture. As infants develop into toddlers and preschoolers, they move toward

- Wider, more complex emotional relationships
- Better coordination and control of emotions and emotion-related skills
- More ability to reflect on their own feelings and those of others
- Representation of emotions through language, play, and fantasy
- Linking individual emotions to culturally valued skills and standards
- An integrated, positive, autonomous, but emotionally connected, sense of self

Again, you might search for examples both in the vignette and in the children you teach. Are you seeing growth in these areas? And are there, for some children, areas of concern?

CONCLUSION

Findings from recent studies of emotional development can help early childhood teachers to construct a more accurate base of professional knowledge. By integrating this research with their own insights from practice, early childhood professionals can expand their ability to understand typical patterns and sequences of emotion-related behavior. With this foundation, professionals may be better able to create appropriate, supportive, and challenging expectations for children's emotional development. To supplement this picture, we need to turn to the factors that influence "typical" emotional development, creating the many variations that professionals encounter in their work with young children. Ilene's classroom will provide the background for Exploration 3.

READINGS FOR FURTHER EXPLORATION

Bowlby, J. (1969). *Attachment and loss*. (Vol. 1). London: Hogarth.
     The foundation of more than 30 years of research on adult-child attachment
     relationships.
Bowlby, J. (1998). *A secure base: Parent-child attachment and healthy human development*. New York: Basic Books.
     A collection of many of the writings of this influential thinker.

Eisenberg, N. (1992). *The caring child*. Cambridge, MA: Harvard University Press.
A readable introduction to the development of empathy and prosocial behavior and ways in which families and teachers can support this development.

Fischer, K. W., Shaver, P. R., & Carnochan, P. (1990). How emotions develop and how they organise development. *Cognition and Emotion, 4*, 81–127.
A detailed presentation of Fischer's model of emotional development, grounded in a neo-Piagetian perspective.

Greenspan, S. I., & Greenspan, N. T. (1985). *First feelings: Milestones in the emotional development of your baby and child*. New York: Viking.
With parents in mind, Greenspan details his understanding of typical developmental milestones and describes interventions when adults have concerns.

Howes, C. (1988). Peer interaction of young children. *Monographs of the Society for Research in Child Development, 53*(1, Serial No. 217).
Describes the results of extended studies in child care centers, focusing on very young children's relationships with, and emotional responses to, other children. Even toddlers are capable of deeper and more lasting bonds of affection than one may have thought.

Hyson, M. C. (1979). Lobster on the sidewalk: Understanding and helping children with fears. *Young Children, 37*, 49–60.
Brief description of typical fears in early childhood, focused on developmental changes and influences.

Saarni, C. (1999). *The development of emotional competence*. New York: Guilford Press.
Saarni presents a detailed overview of how each element of emotional competence develops. Addresses a variety of theories but emphasizes social-cognitive underpinnings of emotional development.

Thompson, R. A. (1994). Emotion regulation: A theme in search of a definition. *Monographs of the Society for Research in Child Development, 59*(2–3, Serial No. 240), 25–52.
A thorough and scholarly presentation of timetables and major influences on this important component of early emotional development.

What Can Influence the Course of Early Emotional Development?

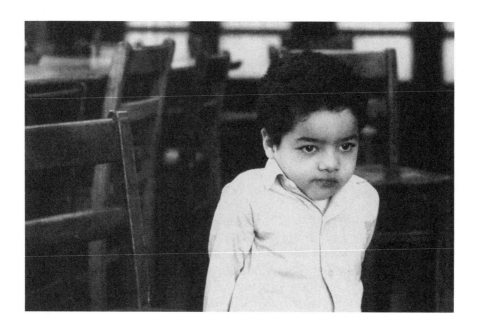

Ilene sits back in her chair, legs crossed, thinking about the year just past. Only 12 months separated the oldest from the youngest child in her Head Start class of 15 four-year-olds, yet their differences seem more striking than their developmental similarities.

"I had a few children this year who absolutely had to have whatever anyone else was using," Ilene recalled. "Charlene was like that. If another child took a book off the bookcase, Charlene *had* to read it; and if she couldn't, it would cause a huge, dramatic crisis for her and everyone around her. She *would* not compromise about what she wanted. It's been interesting to see what has happened recently, though. Because Charlene wants so desperately to be Min's friend, she will give in and make some compromises if that's what it takes to play with her. But she still won't compromise with Kyle—she doesn't care enough about Kyle to make it worth her while."

Ilene's thoughts turn to Spencer, who worried incessantly about any changes in the class routine. "When we have a rainy day," Ilene explained, "we often change our schedule and set up climbers and tunnels inside. The prospect of these changes really bothered Spencer, and he sort of figured out how to deal with it by rehearsing what was going to happen, over and over again. If he even suspected that it might be rainy later on, he'd ask one of the helpers, 'Climbers today, right?' But one answer wasn't good enough for Spencer; he'd keep asking, over and over, as if he were trying to make sure that he had the order straight in his mind. Spencer was the only one who minded having a different schedule on rainy days; but some other children, like Rina, worried about other kinds of changes. The night before our first field trip, Rina told her mother she had a headache and couldn't go to school. Rina's also someone who has a lot of trouble initiating play when some new props have been put out in the classroom.

"That reminds me of something else about the class. There were such differences in the moods of different children. Oh, they all had their unhappy moments, but children like Min just seemed to bubble along, happy and cheerful despite almost anything. Then there was Elon. His face had a scowl a lot of the time. It didn't take much to set him off, yelling and punching. Quiana never got really angry the way Elon did, but more often than not, she's at least mildly unhappy. Other children's unhappiness really bothers Quiana too—she has sometimes started crying if another child is crying, or she'll complain about a stomachache if she hears someone else complaining. It's been a hard year for Quiana; her parents are splitting up and she has been shuttling back and forth between them, but even before that happened, she just seemed like a child who doesn't have a very upbeat feeling about things. Darien also had kind of an unsettled family situation, but his reactions were different. He just pulled away from everyone for a while. Now he's his old perky self."

It's helpful to know about the typical milestones of emotional development, as outlined in Exploration 2. But it is even more important for the effective practitioner to identify the *reasons* for those changes and to recognize the many complex factors that create variations in the pathway of emotional development. By considering the questions and the recommended readings in this exploration, emotion-centered teachers can become even more attuned to the roots of individual developmental patterns and can identify areas where thoughtful, well-timed interventions may help.

1. *Beyond "heredity versus environment."* The old question of whether it is heredity or environment that causes differences in development is not asked today. Instead, the important question is how these two influences work together, in complicated and interactive ways. Consider any of the individual characteristics that Ilene describes, and consider all the potential pathways that can lead to their appearance.

2. *Brain development.* Enormous interest has surrounded findings from "the new brain development research"—even though much of it was done decades ago. Two points are equally important, namely, that brain maturation influences much of what children are capable of emotionally at different ages; and that environment and relationships have powerful influences on brain development, again affecting emotional understanding and control. These influences cannot be observed directly. However, some children's ability to regulate emotions or to understand others' feelings appears to be linked to the kinds of harmful early environments that can compromise brain development, one often-discussed example being children raised in Romanian orphanages. In your own and your colleagues' experience, have you known children who have experienced these kinds of emotionally barren environments? What have been the effects?

3. *Gender.* When you look at the children in Ilene's class, do you see gender differences in the expression of emotions? Many stereotypes exist, and it does appear that in some ways girls may be more tuned into others' feelings. Yet again the influence of biology and environment interact—how do you treat girls' expressions of anger, for example, as compared with boys? And emotional difficulties in young girls may be overlooked, as they more often suppress or "overregulate" their emotions, while boys may show obvious behavioral problems.

4. *Atypical development.* Not all children with disabilities are alike, but having a disability can influence the course of emotional development. Once again, the path is complex: In some cases the disability may have a direct influence on the expression or understanding of emotions, but in other cases the disability may limit opportunities to learn about emotions, because of actual physical limitations or because of adults' assumptions. Knowledgeable teachers can make a great difference. In Ilene's class, Spencer has been diagnosed with attention deficit disorder; can you see how this may be affecting his emotional development, and how Ilene is responding? What other examples do you have from your own experience?

5. *Individual differences in temperament.* Temperament, or behavioral style, appears to be strongly influenced by heredity and is unlikely to change over time. From infancy, children differ in their intensity, inhibition, sociability, adaptability, and in many other dimensions of individual difference. Many of these characteristics are closely related to emotional styles, and can influence children's typical patterns of emotion regulation and expression. In Ilene's class, temperamental differences are striking—Charlene and Kyle are notable examples. Reflect upon these differences

and their possible effects on emotional development and also on how teachers may respond to differing temperaments. To what extent are teachers' responses to children's emotional styles or temperaments influenced by the "fit" with the teacher's own style, or with her preferences for certain kinds of children?

6. *Skills and challenges in other developmental areas.* All areas of development are interconnected. The course of emotional development can be influenced by differences in children's physical, cognitive, language, or social development, creating either opportunities or challenges. Ilene's class had several children whose home language was Spanish and who at the beginning of the year spoke no English. Consider the effect of that language difference on their emotional understanding and communication with other, English-speaking children. Strong social skills, as evidenced in Charlene's friendship with Min, can enrich children's emotional lives as well. And cognitive skills—being able to process information about emotionally-charged situations, for example—make it possible for some children to deal with their emotions more capably. All of this suggests that teachers who actively promote children's competence in *all* areas of development are directly contributing to emotional competence.

7. *Family relationships and environment.* How might the individual differences described by Ilene be traced back to family relationships and the environment of children's families and communities? Earlier chapters emphasized the power of secure relationships, adult modeling, and adults' promotion of "emotion talk." Emotionally open and expressive families tend to have children who also have those characteristics; again, what are examples in the vignette or in your own work? In contrast, mothers' depression, as well as anger and violence within families, can create emotional difficulties for children. Yet children respond differently even under similar stresses, as in the case of Darien and Quiana, and perhaps other children you know.

8. *Cultural influences.* A final, powerful influence on the course of emotional development is culture. Throughout this book, we have seen how culture creates contexts within which children, their families, and their teachers, express emotions and respond to others' feelings. Ilene's class includes children from China, India, Korea, and several Latin American countries, each with distinctive cultural expectations and values. Ilene has found that the Asian children in her class behave less aggressively than many of the other 4-year-olds, and they are also more upset at separation from their mothers; consider how family and cultural socialization might account for these patterns. Ilene has also noted that the three Latino children in her class were especially reluctant to share their own opinions and information at circle time, although each showed this reluctance differently. Over time, Ilene realized that this emotional reticence was related to the children's membership in cultures that stress interdependence and collective identity, rather than individualism. "Putting yourself forward" is dis-

couraged in the children's families, where group welfare comes first, so Ilene needed to change her approach in seeking children's involvement.

Teachers' responses to children's emotions also are influenced by their culture. In one study, for example, Japanese teachers expressed a belief that they ought to let children be physically aggressive. How has your own culture influenced your emotional expectations?

CONCLUSION

In this exploration we have reviewed many factors that affect early emotional development. Children's biological characteristics, temperament, skills in other developmental areas, family environments, and cultures all work together in complex ways to produce the kinds of emotion-related patterns that Ilene saw among her 4-year-olds. The readings recommended below, and the resources listed in the appendices that follow, will further expand your ability to meet these individual needs and promote children's emotional development.

READINGS FOR FURTHER EXPLORATION

Denham, S. (1998). *Emotional development in young children.* New York: Guilford Press.
    Comprehensive, readable discussion that includes a review of what is known about the emotional development of young children with autism and Down syndrome.
Eisenberg, N., & Fabes, R. A. (1992). Emotion regulation and the development of social competence. In M.S. Clark (Ed.), *Review of personality and social psychology: Vol. 14. Emotion and social behavior* (pp. 119–150). Newbury Park, CA: Sage.
    Presents evidence of the connections between temperament characteristics and children's development of emotional and social abilities.
Gottman, J. M., Katz, L. F., & Hooven, C. (1996). *Meta-emotion: How families communicate emotionally, links to child peer relations, and other developmental outcomes.* Mahwah, NJ: Erlbaum.
    Fascinating observations of how families create and communicate beliefs about emotion and how, over time, those beliefs affect children's development.
Kitayama, S., & Markus, H. (Eds.). (1994). *Emotion and culture.* Washington, DC: American Psychological Association.
    Collection of chapters on many aspects of cultural psychology and emotions research, including, but not limited to, the study of young children.
Lemerise, E. A., & Arsenio, W. F. (2000). An integrated model of emotional processes and cognition in social information processing. *Child Development, 71,* 107–118.
    Presents a model of emotional development in which children's information processing skills play a very important part in their ability to understand and respond to emotion.
Lewis, M., & Sullivan, M. E. (1996). *Emotional development in atypical children.* Hillsdale, NJ: Erlbaum.

Chapters focus on a variety of disabilities and developmental delays, summarizing research and implications for intervention.

Lynch, E. W., & Hanson, M. J. (1998). *Developing cross-cultural competence: A guide for working with children and their families.* Baltimore: Paul H. Brookes.

A readable, knowledgeable discussion of the typical characteristics of a number of cultures, as they may affect practitioners' interactions with families. Without stereotyping, the authors provide clear suggestions for respectful relationships that take cultural values into account.

Saarni, C. (1999). *The development of emotional competence.* New York: Guilford Press.

Includes excellent discussions of both gender-related and cultural influences on every aspect of emotional development.

Sandall, S., McLean, M., & Smith, B. (Eds.). (2000). *DEC recommended practices in early intervention/early childhood special education.* Longmont, CO: Sopris West.

Recommendations from a national organization about all aspects of working effectively with young children with disabilities. Includes evidence-based recommendations in the emotional and social areas.

Sharma, D., & Fischer, K. W. (Eds.). (1998). *Socioemotional development across cultures,* New Directions for Child Development, no. 81. San Francisco: Jossey-Bass.

Edited collection of chapters on the complex contexts and pathways of socioemotional development in diverse cultures. Includes a chapter on Reggio Emilia preschools.

Shonkoff, J., & Meisels, S. (Eds.). (2000). *Handbook of early childhood intervention* (2nd ed.). New York: Cambridge University Press.

Excellent collection of chapters describing research-based approaches to helping young children with a variety of developmental challenges, including those in the social and emotional domains.

Early Childhood Education and the Emotion-Focused Tradition: Historical Perspectives

Note: The following discussion complements this book's introduction by providing a historical perspective on the unique features and historical roots of the emotion-focused tradition in early childhood education. It describes examples of this tradition and also describes some early criticisms of early childhood education's emphasis on emotions. References are listed for those interested in learning even more about the history of the early childhood field.

The history of early childhood education can be reconstructed from many sources: oral histories, manuals and guides for practitioners, influential theoretical works, contents of professional journals, and descriptions of past and present teacher education programs. As summarized in several comprehensive historical accounts (e.g., Lascarides & Hinitz, 2000; Osborn, 1991; Weber, 1984), programs for young children have varied greatly in their philosophical foundations, curriculum content, and teaching practices. Other writers (e.g., Chung & Walsh, 2000) have added postmodern and critical perspectives to these accounts. Despite the field's variability, certain patterns seem to have recurred over the long history of early childhood education, forming what might be considered a "core tradition."

UNIQUE HISTORICAL FEATURES

A concern with emotions goes beyond early childhood education, of course; teachers and researchers in elementary and secondary education have certainly not ignored emotional development. However, the history of early childhood education contains several unique features that help to account for the field's emotion-focused character.

Early Philosophical Roots

While acknowledging competing philosophies and influences, historical accounts of early childhood education find its strongest philosophical roots in the European romantic tradition (Kohlberg & Mayer, 1972; Weber, 1984). In literature as well as in life, romanticism viewed "feeling" as the wellspring of human endeavor

and valued spontaneous expressions of natural impulses. Froebel, generally regarded as the father of early childhood education, developed a set of mystical beliefs that had strong links with the idealistic, romantic philosophies of his time. His
educational approach encouraged the outward expression of the child's inner feelings and thoughts; by this means, Froebel thought, the child would be brought into
a fundamental sense of unity with the divine.

Independent Origins of Early Childhood Education Programs

Another factor that may have contributed to the field's emphasis on emotion is that programs for young children originated apart from formal systems of
public education. Child care, nursery schools, and kindergartens began independent of bureaucratic institutions and responded to needs broader than the acquisition of academic skills (Shapiro, 1983; Weber, 1969). Although in most parts of the
U.S. kindergartens became integrated with public elementary schools by the 1920s,
several writers have argued that their early history allowed them to be more open
to new psychological ideas (Katz, 1971; Weber, 1969). Beane's (1990) historical review of the rocky path of "affect" in public education offers convincing evidence
that emotion issues were more easily accepted in early childhood settings than in
elementary and secondary public schools.

Psychological Underpinnings of Early Childhood Education

Beginning in the 1920s, psychoanalysis made a significant impact on the
thinking of early childhood practitioners through its emphasis on the power of
subconscious emotions to motivate behavior and learning. Gesell's normative picture of child development also may have contributed to this emotion-focused tradition (Gesell, Ilg, & Ames, 1943/1974). Many early childhood educators began to
adopt a belief in allowing free expression to children's "natural" behavior as it
unfolded in predetermined stages. Since that time, these theoretical perspectives
have been used as psychological underpinnings for many early childhood programs
and popular texts in early childhood education.

EXAMPLES OF THE EMOTION-FOCUSED TRADITION

Largely because of these unique historical factors, an emphasis on children's
emotional development has been a central feature of the core tradition in early
childhood education. Numerous books, articles, and program models have reflected
this tradition. Weber (1984) provides a thorough, scholarly overview of the effects
of Freudian, neo-Freudian, and maturationist theories on teacher education and
early childhood curriculum. Rather than attempting to summarize this and other
accounts, I will briefly illustrate the emotion-focused tradition with a few repre-
sentative examples from the history of twentieth-century American early childhood
education. In each of these examples, emotions take center stage as the central influence on children's development and learning.

Psychodynamic Influences

In the 1920s, many nursery school educators looked to Freud's theory to understand and guide the development of children under the age of 5. The City and Country School in New York City was established in 1913 by Caroline Pratt and was sponsored by the Bureau of Educational Experiments, later known as the Bank Street College of Education. Those involved in the Bureau also included Lucy Sprague Mitchell and Harriet Johnson. Johnson's (1928) book, *Children in the Nursery School*, reflects the viewpoint that children's development is strongly social and affective and that teachers should expect strong expressions of emotion in young children.

By the 1940s, neo-Freudian and maturationist theories converged to produce an unprecedented level of interest in children's emotional development (Weber, 1984). One outgrowth of this interest was the formation of the Teachers' Service Committee on the Emotional Needs of Children. Formed in the years immediately after World War II, the committee was chaired by Lawrence Frank, who had become a major influence on the field's attention to emotion issues.

One of the many publications from the committee was a down-to-earth pamphlet for teachers of young children, *A Pound of Prevention: How Teachers Can Meet the Emotional Needs of Young Children*, written by committee member James Hymes (1947). In this pamphlet and in many other writings, Hymes stressed the fundamental importance of the teacher's emotional relationship with children. "Smile when your children come to school in the morning," he urged. "Put your arm around his shoulder or hold his hand. . . . Be just as generous as you know how with honest interest and appreciation" (p. 21).

Concerned especially with children damaged by the emotional stresses of the war years, Hymes used a psychodynamic metaphor to make his point that "everyone has angry feelings bottled up inside of him" (p. 27). Hymes recommended that teachers help children cope with their feelings by offering "safety valves" such as clay, punching bags, and pretend play, and that teachers talk openly with children about their feelings.

A second example from the post–World War II era was the appearance of *Understanding Children's Play* (Hartley, Frank, & Goldenson, 1952). This widely cited book, the result of another project guided by Lawrence Frank, compiled and interpreted play observations in scores of nursery schools and kindergartens, using a psychodynamic perspective. The authors used these observations to support the idea that play is both a window into children's emotional lives and an avenue by which children can express and master their feelings. The authors urged that negative emotions be recognized by teachers and allowed safe outlets: "Instead of making children feel guilty about destructive impulses, the teacher might do them a great service by arranging a 'throwing corner' [for blocks], with a piece of heavy wallboard to receive the blows" (p. 49).

The history of what is now the Bank Street College of Education reflects a unique attempt to integrate an explicitly psychoanalytic perspective with cognitive developmental theory. From its beginnings in 1916 as Lucy Sprague Mitchell's Bureau of Educational Experiments, Bank Street advocated early childhood programs that promoted the integration and interaction of "cognitive-intellectual and affective-social processes" (Biber, 1942/1984, p. 291). The following statement typifies this emphasis: "Affect, sensation, wonder, thinking—the child's experience is a rich composite of all of them, and his education should be a rich response to all of them" (p. 16).

Biber described Bank Street's "developmental-interaction approach" as having been strongly influenced by psychoanalysis (particularly ego psychology), by the progressive education movement, and by the preventive mental health orientation promulgated by Lawrence Frank and others, as well as by the cognitive theories of Jean Piaget. As seen through these lenses, emotion has a broad set of functions. Like other psychoanalytically oriented early childhood programs, the Bank Street model acknowledged that children need to express their negative feelings. However, Biber also stressed the positive emotional bases of children's self-initiated learning: "satisfied curiosity, the pleasures and intrinsic rewards of mastery, identification with teacher figures, and the internalizations of the trusted adults' confidence in the child's competence" (p. 290). The cognitive-affective perspective embodied in Biber's words has been a major influence on early childhood teacher preparation and recommendations for classroom practices.

Open Education

The 1970s brought another upsurge of interest in the emotional aspects of young children's education. Influenced by British primary education, the "open education" movement fostered a renewed attention to emotions in American public and private schools (Nyquist & Hawes, 1972). From Isaacs (1930/1963) and other sources, educators constructed an approach that emphasized child-initiated projects using home and neighborhood experiences. Open education practitioners used children's own experiences as the raw materials for the curriculum partly because they believed these events' emotional power would motivate learning and intellectual engagement. Open education also valued the emotional quality of classroom interactions. Children were expected to be direct and spontaneous. Both positive and negative feelings were valued and encouraged: "Since significant growth is expected to be accompanied by a wide range of emotions . . . at times children will become not only joyful but quite unsettled, doubtful, perhaps anxious" (Bussis & Chittenden, 1972, pp. 134–135).

Affective Education

A second widely influential movement in the 1970s was "affective education." Shaped by humanistic psychology, the affective education movement attempted to incorporate explicit emotion-related activities into the curriculum of elementary and secondary schools. Although less directly applied to preschool programs, the movement's goals held wide appeal. Affective education aimed to encourage children to express their feelings in the classroom and to develop a curriculum that would help children understand their own and others' feelings.

A number of writers offered teachers specific activities intended to stimulate children's empathy, their ability to label emotions, and their capacity to express emotions in a direct, authentic way. A book titled *Left-Handed Teaching: Lessons in Affective Education* (Castillo, 1974) exemplifies this approach. Castillo's introductory chapter acknowledges the influence of humanistic and Gestalt psychologists, including Maslow, Rogers, May, and Jourard. "Confluent education" is advocated as a way to permit the child "to develop his emotional abilities along with his intellectual abilities" (p. 13). As outlined by Castillo, the affective curriculum would consist of emotion-related lessons or activities organized around thematic units, including "Imagination," "Sensory Awareness," "Communication," "Aggression," and "Building Trust." The book's description of the unit on aggression shows that the direct expression of feelings is valued: One goal is "to be able to experience anger where and when it occurs" (p. 137). Like most other proponents of affective education, Castillo also emphasizes the appropriate socialization of emotions: "to know when and where anger can be expressed, and to express it at appropriate times and places" (p. 137).

CRITICISMS OF THE EMOTION-FOCUSED TRADITION

These historical examples illustrate how emotion-related beliefs have influenced early childhood programs. However, this emphasis on the importance of emotions and emotional development did not go unchallenged. A focus on emotions often was regarded as dangerous to children's intellectual growth or as a fuzzily romantic residue of an earlier time.

Criticisms During the Early Kindergarten Movement

Even in the earliest days of the Froebelian kindergarten movement in the United States, tension arose between those favoring a stronger emphasis on emotion and those with a more "rational" or academic bent. Shapiro's (1983) history of the American kindergarten movement described Elizabeth Peabody chiding public kindergarten founders William Harris and Susan Blow for overemphasizing rationality in kindergarten education, while Harris responded by warning that the "gushing hilarity" of children schooled in the practices of romantic Froebelians would limit their intellectual development.

Criticisms from the 1960s' Cognitive Revolution

The cognitive revolution of the 1960s brought strong criticisms of "traditional" early childhood educators' focus on emotional and social development. Deutsch (1967), for example, asserted:

> The overgeneralized influence on some sections of early childhood education of the emphasis in the child guidance movement upon protecting the child from stress, creating a supportive environment, and resolving emotional conflicts has done more to misdirect and retard the fields of child care, guidance, and development than any other single influence. (pp. 73–74)

Evans's (1975) summary of the 1960s' upsurge of interest in early childhood education labeled the renewed emphasis on cognition as the most significant trend of the decade. He emphasized the sharp disagreements between traditional adherents to social-emotional curricula and the "newer" proponents of a cognitive emphasis. Further, Evans characterized open education and informal education movements as having ill-formed goals and narrow perspectives. Evans argued that traditional early childhood educators cast cognitively focused programs in the worst possible light, assuming that their adherents must be "cold, authoritarian, rigid, and therefore 'bad'" while their own approach was "warm, open, flexible, and therefore 'good'" (p. 281).

CONCLUSION

Obviously, these debates and their often-polarized views of cognition and emotion have recurred in the past 2 decades. The emotion-focused core tradition in early childhood education and the recurring criticisms of that tradition provide a backdrop for the decline and strong resurgence of interest in early emotional development in the late twentieth and early twenty-first centuries—trends described in this book's Introduction.

FOR FURTHER READING

Beatty, B. (1995). *Preschool education in America: The culture of young children from the colonial era to the present.* New Haven, CT: Yale University Press.

Chung, S., & Walsh, D. J. (2000). Unpacking "child-centeredness": A history of meanings. *Journal of Curriculum Studies, 32,* 215–234.

Gesell, A., Ilg, F. L., & Ames, L. B. (1995). *Infant and child in the culture of today: The guidance of development in home and nursery school.* Northvale, NJ: Jason Aronson. (Original work published 1943)

Goffin, S. G. (2001). Whither early childhood education in the next century? *Education across a century: The centennial volume* (pp. 140–163), National Society for the Study of Education. Chicago: University of Chicago Press.

Lascarides, V. C., & Hinitz, B. F. (2000). *History of early childhood education.* New York: Falmer Press.

Osborn, D. K. (1991). *Early childhood education in historical perspective* (3rd ed.). Athens, GA: Daye Press.

Weber, E. (1984). *Ideas influencing early childhood education: A theoretical analysis.* New York: Teachers College Press.

Intervention Programs to Support Emotional Competence

SELECTING INTERVENTION PROGRAMS: SOME GUIDELINES

This appendix offers selected examples of classroom-level interventions (in some cases with a family component) designed to support young children's emotional competence. Evaluations have shown at least some positive effects for each. Some interventions have been focused on children in kindergarten and first grade; fewer focus on children before kindergarten. Brief descriptions of the programs' characteristics are provided, followed by Web sites and other references for further information (including details of evaluations). Several points should be kept in mind when considering or adopting any intervention or prevention program (adapted from Raver, 2002):

• High-quality early education, including a rich, emotion-focused curriculum, provides the foundation to which programs such as this may be added. Caring, emotionally knowledgeable teachers and a classroom climate that addresses and integrates the goals emphasized in this book are essential.

• Research indicates that the most effective emotional-competence programs go beyond commercial packages that simply teach children names for feelings and that encourage children to "use words" to resolve conflicts. At least with elementary-age children, such programs are relatively ineffective when used in isolation (Raver & Knitzer, 2002). Effective programs require investment in professional development; link classroom lessons with games or other activities to build self-control and other skills; and coordinate classroom-level interventions with parent training and support. As compared with more limited interventions, such programs are expensive, but research indicates that the investment is worthwhile (Raver & Knitzer, 2002).

• An approach that has shown very positive results is to combine universal programs (for all children in a classroom or school) with more intensive intervention, in school and with families, for a smaller number of children who seem to be at greater risk for emotional difficulties.

• Although the programs described below have shown positive results, evaluation data need to be considered in the light of each specific situation. How similar is the school or center's setting to those in which the program has been used and evaluated? Are the outcomes that were evaluated ones that are considered important?

• High-intensity clinical interventions, perhaps using school-based early childhood mental health consultants, are recommended for young children at high risk of serious emotional problems, often because of family adversity (Kauffman Early Education Exchange, 2002). However, such interventions must avoid inappropriate labeling or stigmatizing of children and, again, must address family needs as well as those of individual children.

SELECTED EXAMPLES OF PROGRAMS

Fast Track

Program developer. Conduct Problems Prevention Research Group

Fast Track is a comprehensive, multisite intervention designed to prevent serious and chronic antisocial behavior in a sample of children selected as high-risk at school entry because of their conduct problems in kindergarten and home. All children in a classroom receive an extended social and emotional skills curriculum (the PATHS curriculum, see below), while a smaller number of kindergarteners who already show behavioral problems receive more intensive intervention with their families, including academic as well as social and emotional intervention. (Not commercially available)

For more information. http://www.fasttrackproject.org/default.htm

McMahon, R. J., & Conduct Problems Prevention Research Group. (in press). The prevention of conduct problems using targeted and universal interventions: The Fast Track Program. In D. Offord (Ed.), *Prevention of conduct disorder.* New York: Cambridge University Press.

Floor Time

Program developer. Stanley Greenspan, M.D.

Also termed the Developmental Individual-Difference, Relationship-Based Model (DIR), the Floor Time approach focuses on helping all children—but especially those with disabilities such as autism—develop relationships and emotional communication. The goals of the one-on-one Floor Time intervention are to help the child become more alert, take more initiative, become more flexible, tolerate frustration, sequence and execute actions, communicate gesturally and verbally, and take pleasure in learning. Parents and other adults learn how to use individual interactions with a child (with or without disabilities) to support these goals.

For more information. http://www.stanleygreenspan.com

Greenspan, S. I., & Weider, S. (1998). *The child with special needs: Encouraging intellectual and emotional growth.* Reading, MA: Addison-Wesley.

The Incredible Years

Program developer. Carolyn Webster-Stratton, Ph.D., University of Washington

The Incredible Years intervention offers comprehensive training for parents, teachers, and children ages 3–8, focused on improving children's emotional and behavioral adjustment. Programs include videotapes, activities for parents and children, and other school- and home-based materials. Empathy, problem solving, and anger management are among the areas of emphasis for children. (Evaluated in Head Start settings.)

For more information. *http://www.incredibleyears.com*
Webster-Stratton, C., Reid, M. J., & Hammond, M. (2001). Preventing conduct problems, promoting social competence: A parent and teacher training partnership in Head Start. *Journal of Child Clinical Psychology*, 30, 283–302.

Paths

Program developer. Mark Greenberg, Ph.D., Penn State Prevention Research Center

PATHS (Providing Alternative Thinking Strategies) was developed for elementary school and adapted for preschool (Preschool PATHS), where it was tested in Head Start programs. Using PATHS characters and other tools, curriculum units teach self-regulation (the Turtle Technique), emotion awareness and communication, problem solving, positive identity, and peer relations. It also promotes a positive classroom atmosphere to support social-emotional learning.

For more information. *http://www.prevention.psu.edu/PATHS/index.html*
Kusché, C. A., & Greenberg, M. T. (in press). PATHS in your classroom: Promoting emotional literacy and alleviating emotional distress. In J. Cohen (Ed.), *Social emotional learning and the elementary school child: A guide for educators*. New York: Teachers College Press.

Second Step: A Violence Prevention Curriculum

Program developer. Committee for Children, Seattle, WA

Second Step is a social and emotional skills curriculum using photographs with classroom discussion, role-plays, adult modeling, sing-alongs, and schoolwide reinforcement. With 20 lessons for each grade level from preschool through ninth grade, the program aims to develop emotional understanding, empathy, impulse control, problem solving, and anger management. A companion program is used with families of Second Step students. Program developers link Second Step curriculum to Head Start performance standards.

For more information. *http://www.cfchildren.org*
Grossman, D. C., Neckerman, H. J., Koepsell, T. D., Liu, P.–Y., Asher, K. N., Beland, K., Frey, K., & Rivara, F. P. (1997). Effectiveness of a violence prevention curriculum among children in elementary school: A randomized controlled trial. *Journal of the American Medical Association*, 277, 1605–1611.

Social-Emotional Intervention Program

Program developer. Susanne Denham, Ph.D., George Mason University

Incorporating components from a number of other prevention and intervention efforts—PATHS' Turtle Technique (Kusche & Greenberg, 1994), Floor Time (Greenspan & Weider, 1998), I Can Problem Solve (Shure, 1992)—the program trains child care teachers to implement activities focused on relationship building, emotional understanding, emotion regulation, and social problem solving. The emphasis included spontaneous as well as planned activities and the creation of opportunities for dialogue and modeling. (Not commercially available.)

For more information.

Burton, R., & Denham, S. A. (1998). "Are you my friend?" How two young children learned to get along with others. *Journal of Research in Childhood Education, 12,* 210–223.

Denham, S. A., & Burton, R. (1996). A social-emotional intervention for at-risk four-year-olds. *Journal of School Psychology, 34,* 225–245.

Supporting the Head Start Child Outcomes Framework Through an Emotion-Centered Curriculum

The Head Start Child Outcomes Framework (Head Start Bureau, 2001) describes expectations for children's learning and development in eight domains. Although an emotionally focused program can support learning in all domains (see Chapter 1), the content presented in this book is especially relevant for two important Head Start domains: Social and Emotional Development and Approaches to Learning. The following chart suggests how specific chapters of this book, and the goals for emotional development they describe, are linked to the indicators in these domains.

Domain	Domain Element	Indicators	Supportive Material from this Book
Social and Emotional Development	Self-Concept	Begins to develop and express awareness of self in terms of specific abilities, characteristics, and preferences.	Chapters 3 and 6
		Develops growing capacity for independence in a range of activities, routines, and tasks.	Chapter 2
		Demonstrates growing confidence in a range of abilities and expresses pride in accomplishments.	Chapters 2, 6, and 7
	Self-Control	Shows progress in expressing feelings, needs, and opinions in difficult situations and conflicts without harming self, others, or property.	Chapters 4 and 5
		Develops growing understanding of how their actions affect others and begins to accept the consequences of actions.	Chapters 3 and 5
		Demonstrates increasing capacity to follow rules and routines and use materials purposefully, safely, and respectfully.	Chapter 5
	Cooperation	Increases abilities to sustain interactions with peers by helping, sharing, and discussion.	Chapter 3
		Shows increasing abilities to use compromise and discussion in working, playing, and resolving conflicts with peers.	Chapters 4 and 5
		Develops increasing abilities to give and take in interactions, to take turns in games or using materials, and to interact without being overly submissive or directive.	Chapter 5
	Social Relationships	Demonstrates increasing comfort in talking with and accepting guidance and directions from a range of familiar adults.	Chapter 2
		Shows progress in developing friendships with peers.	Chapters 2 and 3
		Progresses in responding sympathetically to peers who are in need, upset, hurt, or angry, and in expressing empathy or caring for others.	Chapters 3 and 6

Domain	Domain Element	Indicators	Supportive Material from this Book
Social and Emotional Development (*continued*)	Knowledge of Families and Communities	Develops ability to identify personal characteristics, including gender and family composition.	Chapter 6
		Progresses in understanding similarities and respecting differences among people, such as genders, race, special needs, culture, language, and family structures.	Chapters 3 and 6
		Develops growing awareness of jobs and what is required to perform them.	
		Begins to express and understand concepts and language of geography in the contexts of classroom, home, and community.	
Approaches to Learning	Initiative and Curiosity	Chooses to participate in an increasing variety of tasks and activities.	Chapter 7
		Develops increased ability to make independent choices.	Chapters 2 and 7
		Approaches tasks and activities with increased flexibility, imagination, and inventiveness.	Chapters 2 and 7
		Grows in eagerness to learn about and discuss a growing range of topics, ideas and tasks.	Chapter 7
	Engagement and Persistence	Grows in abilities to persist in and complete a variety of tasks, activities, projects, and experiences.	Chapters 2, 5, and 7
		Demonstrates increasing ability to set goals and develop and follow through on plans.	Chapters 5 and 7
		Shows growing capacity to maintain concentration over time on a task, question, set of directions, or interactions, despite distractions and interruptions.	Chapters 5 and 7
	Reasoning and Problem Solving	Develops increasing ability to find more than one solution to a question, task, or problem.	Chapters 5 and 7
		Grows in recognizing and solving problems through active exploration, including trial and error, and interactions and discussions with peers and adults.	Chapters 4, 5, and 7
		Develops increasing abilities to classify, compare, and contrast objects, events, and experiences.	Chapters 3 and 7

Tools to Assess Young Children's Emotional Development

GENERAL ASSESSMENT GUIDELINES

Good assessment, including ongoing, classroom-based assessment of children's emotional development, is an essential teaching tool. References at the end of this appendix provide guidelines for early childhood assessment, emphasizing the importance of embedding assessment in ongoing activities, avoiding reliance on a single assessment tool, and taking care to use assessments only for the purposes for which they were developed (for example, not using a screening tool to make decisions about children's placement in programs).

Professional judgment is needed to select appropriate assessment tools. In making these judgments, consider how well the instruments connect with your own goals and your goals for children—in general, and in the area of emotional development. In assessing emotional development, look for tools that go beyond identifying problems, or that go beyond defining emotional competence simply as the absence of negative behaviors. Rather, seek out tools to help you identify and build on children's growing competencies.

Some emotion-related assessment tools may be used by knowledgeable classroom teachers without specific training. Other tools require training; still others require collaboration with specialists to interpret and use results. Review the instruments' descriptions carefully.

ASSESSMENT OF EMOTIONAL DEVELOPMENT WITHIN OTHER CURRICULUM AND ASSESSMENT SYSTEMS

A number of broad curriculum and assessment systems pay a good deal of attention to emotional, or sometimes socioemotional, development. A few examples are listed here.

Creative Curriculum for Early Childhood (Dodge & Colker, 2002)
Using activity or interest areas in the classroom, the Creative Curriculum aims to support development in three areas including socioemotional development. Assessments include children's portfolios and Child Development and Learning Checklists.
Sample Items: "Demonstrates confidence in growing abilities"; Demonstrates increasing independence"—rated several times during the year as "Not yet; Sometimes; Regularly."

High/Scope Child Observation Record (COR) (High/Scope Staff, 1992)
Implementation of the High/Scope curriculum includes the use of anecdotal notecards, portfolios, and teacher ratings of children's levels of accomplishment using the COR. Initiative and Social Relations are two of six domains assessed with the COR.
Sample Items: "Understanding and expressing feelings"—rated on one of five levels from "Child does not yet express or verbalize feelings" to "Child responds appropriately to the feelings of others." Teachers rate this and other areas three times during the year.

Work Sampling System (WSS) (Meisels, Liaw, Dorfman, and Nelson, 1995)
Not a curriculum in itself, the Work Sampling System is compatible with a variety of curriculum approaches. Focus is on authentic assessment using samples of children's work. Teachers complete Developmental Checklists four times a year, in areas including Personal and Social Development.
Sample Items: "Shows comfort and confidence with self"; "Shows eagerness and curiosity as a learner"; "Shows empathy and caring for others." Teachers rate as "Not Yet," "In Progress," or "Proficient."

SPECIFIC ASSESSMENT OF EMOTIONAL DEVELOPMENT AND EMOTIONAL COMPETENCE

The following are examples of tools developed specifically to assess aspects of early emotional development and competence.

Adjustment Scale for Preschool Intervention (Lutz, Fantuzzo, & McDermott, 2002)
Teachers complete descriptions of children's adaptive and maladaptive responses to 24 routine early childhood classroom situations. Developed in collaboration with Head Start personnel, it is used in Head Start settings to help identify children with emotional and behavioral needs.
Sample Items: How does this child cope with new learning tasks? (teachers check all that apply)

- Has a happy-go-lucky attitude to every problem
- Charges in without taking time to think or follow instructions
- Approaches new tasks with caution, but tries
- Won't even attempt it if he/she senses a difficulty
- Likes the challenge of something difficult
- Cannot work up the energy to face anything new

Ages and Stages Questionnaire: Social-Emotional (Squires, Bricker, & Twombly, 2001)
Parents rate children's functioning in seven areas: self-regulation, compliance, communication, adaptive functioning, autonomy, affect, and interaction with people. Professionals evaluate scores.

Sample Items: "Can your child settle himself down after periods of exciting activity?"; "Does your child let you know how he is feeling either with words or gestures?"; "Does your child cling to you more than you expect?"

Emotion Regulation Checklist (Shields & Cicchetti, 1998)
This checklist is designed to be completed by teachers, parents, or others familiar with a child. Items are rated on a 4-point scale from "Never" to "Almost Always" and assess emotional intensity, negativity, flexibility, appropriateness to the situation, and so on. Frequently used for research purposes, it has been used in Head Start settings.

Sample Items: "Can recover quickly from episodes of upset or distress"; "Can modulate excitement in emotionally arousing situations"; "Displays exuberance that others find intrusive or disruptive"; "Displays negative emotions when attempting to engage others in play."

Hawaii Early Learning Profile (HELP) (Parks, 1997)
HELP was designed to assist in program planning for young children who are at risk or have disabilities and developmental delays. One of six developmental domains is the Social-Emotional strand, including checklists and charts for Attachment/Separation/Autonomy, Development of Self, Expression of Emotions and Feelings, Learning Rule and Expectations, and Social Interactions and Play. Items appropriate from birth to age 3, as well as from 3 to 6, are provided with detailed descriptions. It is best used in consultation with other professionals and specialists.

Sample Items: "Expresses affection"; "Attempts to comfort others in distress"; "Experiences difficulty with transitions"; "Enjoys a wide range of relationships"; "Dramatizes feelings using a doll."

Social Competence and Behavior Evaluation, Preschool Edition (SCBE) (LaFreniere & Dumas, 1995)
Teachers rate children on the basis of observed classroom behavior. Used in Head Start settings and in multinational research, the SCBE describes children's behavior for purposes of socialization and education, but is not intended for diagnosis. It provides assessment of social competence (joyful, secure, prosocial, and so on), emotional expression, and adjustment.

Sample Items: "Comforts or assists another child in difficulty"; "Attentive toward younger children"; "Accepts compromises when reasons are given"; "Easily frustrated."

ASSESSMENT RESOURCES

Bagnato, S. J., Neisworth, J. T., & Munson, S. M. (1997). *LINKing assessment and early intervention: An authentic curriculum-based approach.* Baltimore: Paul H. Brookes.
> Comprehensive descriptions and ratings of curriculum-linked assessments in all areas, with an emphasis on assessment of children with disabilities.

Landy, S. (2002). *Pathways to competence: Encouraging healthy social and emotional development in young children.* Baltimore: Paul H. Brookes.

Comprehensive resource and reference that includes descriptions of selected assessments in areas including emotion regulation and prosocial behavior.

McAfee, O., & Leong, D. (2002). *Assessing and guiding young children's development and learning* (3rd ed.). Boston: Allyn & Bacon.

Extensive, practical introduction to assessment for classroom teachers.

National Association for the Education of Young Children (NAEYC) and National Association of Early Childhood Specialists in State Departments of Education (NAECS/SDE). (2003). *Early childhood curriculum, child assessment, and program evaluation.* Washington, DC: Author.

Assessment guidelines reflect consensus among many experts in the early childhood field and beyond.

Shepard, L. A., Kagan, S. L., & Wurtz, E. (Eds.). (1998). *Principles and recommendations for early childhood assessments.* Washington, DC: National Education Goals Panel.

Addresses assessment and accountability in light of the "Readiness" goal of the National Education Goals Panel (NEGP).

References

Ainsworth, M. D. S., Blehar, M. C., Waters, E., & Wall, S. (1978). *Patterns of attachment*. Hillsdale, NJ: Erlbaum.

Andrews, A., & Trafton, P. R. (2002). *Little kids—powerful problem solvers: Math stories from a kindergarten classroom*. Portsmouth, NH: Heinemann.

Andrews, J. D., & Washington, V. (Eds.). (1998). *Children of 2010*. Washington, DC: NAEYC.

Ayers, W. (1989). *The good preschool teacher*. New York: Teachers College Press.

Bagnato, S. J., Neisworth, J. T., & Munson, S. M. (1997). *LINKing assessment and early intervention: An authentic curriculum-based approach*. Baltimore: Paul H. Brookes.

Bandura, A. (1977). *Social learning theory*. Englewood Cliffs, NJ: Prentice-Hall.

Bandura, A. (1986). *Social foundations of thought and action: A social cognitive theory*. Englewood Cliffs, NJ: Prentice-Hall.

Baratta-Lorton, M. (1994). *Math their way: Complete revised anniversary edition*. Parsippany, NJ: Pearson Learning.

Beane, J. A. (1990). Affect in the curriculum: Toward democracy, dignity, and diversity. New York: Teachers College Press.

Beatty, B. (1995). *Preschool education in America: The culture of young children from the colonial era to the present*. New Haven, CT: Yale University Press.

Bell, K. (1998). Family expressiveness and attachment. *Social Development, 7*(1), 37–53.

Berk, L., & Winsler, A. (1995). *Scaffolding children's learning: Vygotsky and early childhood education*. Washington, DC: NAEYC.

Biber, B. (1984). *Early education and psychological development*. New Haven, CT: Yale University Press. (Original work published 1942)

Blackford, J. U., & Walden, T. A. (1998). Individual differences in social referencing. *Infant Behavior and Development, 21*(1), 89–102.

Blair, C. (2002). School readiness: Integrating cognition and emotion in a neurobiological conceptualization of children's functioning at school entry. *American Psychological Association, 57*(2), 111–127.

Bodrova, E., & Leong, D. J. (1995). *Tools of the mind: A Vygotskian approach to early childhood education*. New York: Prentice-Hall.

Bodrova, E., & Leong, D. J. (2003). Chopsticks and counting chips: Do play and foundational skills need to complete for the teacher's attention in an early childhood classroom? *Young Children, 58*(3), 10–17.

Bowlby, J. (1969). *Attachment and loss* (Vol. 1). London: Hogarth.

Bowlby, J. (1998). *A secure base: Parent-child attachment and healthy human development*. New York: Basic Books.

Bowman, B. (1999). Kindergarten practices with children from low-income families. In R. C. Pianta & M. J. Cox (Eds.), *The transition to kindergarten* (pp. 281–301). Baltimore: Paul H. Brookes.

Bowman, B., Donovan, M. S., & Burns, M. S. (Eds.). (2001). *Eager to learn: Educating our preschoolers.* Washington, DC: National Academy Press.

Bransford, J., Brown, A. L., & Cocking, R. R. (Eds.). (2000). *How people learn: Brain, mind, experience, and school* (Expanded ed.). Washington, DC: National Academy Press.

Brazelton, T. B. (1992). *Touchpoints: Your child's emotional and behavioral development.* Cambridge, MA: Perseus.

Bredekamp, S., & Copple, C. (Eds.). (1997). *Developmentally appropriate practice in early childhood programs* (Rev. ed.). Washington, DC: NAEYC.

Bredekamp, S., & Rosegrant, T. (Eds.). (1992). *Reaching potentials: Appropriate curriculum and assessment for young children* (Vol. 1). Washington, DC: NAEYC.

Burton, R., & Denham, S. A. (1998). "Are you my friend?" How two young children learned to get along with others. *Journal of Research in Childhood Education, 12*(2), 210–223.

Bussis, A. M., & Chittenden, E. A. (1972). Toward clarifying the teacher's role. In E. B. Nyquist & G. R. Hawes (Eds.), *Open education* (pp. 117–136). New York: Bantam.

California Department of Education, Child Development Division. (2001). *Desired results for children and families program summary.* Sacramento, CA: Author. [Online: *http://www.cde.ca.gov/cyfsbranch/child_development/dr2.htm*]

Camras, L., Sachs-Alter, E., & Riborday, S. C. (1996). Emotion understanding in maltreated children: Recognition of facial expressions and integration with other emotion cues. In M. Lewis & M. W. Sullivan (Eds.), *Emotional development in atypical children* (pp. 203–225). Hillsdale, NJ: Erlbaum.

Case, R., Hayward, S., Lewis, M., & Hurst, P. (1988). Toward a neo-Piagetian theory of affective and cognitive development. *Developmental Review, 8*(2), 1–51.

Cassidy, J., & Shaver, P. R. (Eds.). (1999). *Handbook of attachment: Theory, research, and clinical applications.* New York: Guilford.

Castillo, G. A. (1974). *Left-handed teaching: Lessons in affective education.* New York: Praeger.

Chaille, C., & Britain, L. (1997). *The young child as scientist: A constructivist approach to early childhood science education.* New York: Longman.

Chisholm, K. (1998). Three-year follow-up of attachment and indiscriminate friendliness in children adopted from Romanian orphanages. *Child Development, 69*(4), 1092–1106.

Chung, S., & Walsh, D. J. (2000). Unpacking "child-centeredness": A history of meanings. *Journal of Curriculum Studies, 32*(2), 215–234.

Cicchetti, D., & Carlson, V. (Eds.). (1989). *Child maltreatment: Theory and research on the causes and consequences of child abuse and neglect.* Cambridge, UK: Cambridge University Press.

Cicchetti, D., Ganiban, J., & Barnett, D. (1991). Contributions from the study of high-risk populations to understanding the development of emotion regulation. In J. Garber & K. A. Dodge (Eds.), *The development of emotion regulation and dysregulation* (pp. 15–48). New York: Cambridge University Press.

Cicchetti, D., & Hesse, P. (1983). Affect and intellect: Piaget's contributions to the study of infant emotional development. In R. Plutchik & H. Kellerman (Eds.), *Emotion: Theory, research, and experience: Vol. 2. Emotions in early development* (pp. 115–170). New York: Academic Press.

Coates, G. D., & Stenmark, J. K. (1997). *Family math for young children: Comparing.* Berkeley, CA: Lawrence Hall of Science.

Copley, J. V. (Ed.). (1999). *Mathematics in the early years.* Washington, DC: NAEYC.

Copley, J. V. (2000). *The young child and mathematics.* Washington, DC: NAEYC.

Copple, C. (Ed.). (2003). *A world of difference: Readings on teaching young children in a diverse society.* Washington, DC: NAEYC.

Cost, Quality, and Child Outcomes Study Team. (1995). *Cost, quality, and child outcomes in child care centers.* Denver: University of Colorado at Denver.

Davidson, J. I. (1996). *Emergent literacy and dramatic play in early education.* Albany, NY: Delmar.

Denham, S. (1998). *Emotional development in young children.* New York: Guilford Press.

Denham, S. A., & Burton, R. (1996). A social-emotional intervention for at-risk four-year-olds. *Journal of School Psychology, 34*(3), 225–245.

Denham, S., Lehman, E. B., Moser, M. H., & Reeves, S. (1995). Continuity and change in emotional components of temperament. *Child Study Journal, 25,* 289–304.

Denham, S., Mason, T., Caverly, S., Schmidt, M., Hackney, R., Caswell, C., & DeMulder, E. (2001). Preschoolers at play: Co-socialisers of emotional and social competence. *International Journal of Behavioral Development, 25*(4), 290–301.

Derman-Sparks, L., & A.B.C. Task Force. (1989). *Anti-bias curriculum: Tools for empowering young children.* Washington, DC: NAEYC.

Deutsch, M. (1967). *The disadvantaged child.* New York: Basic Books.

DeVries, R., Zan, B., Hildebrandt, C., Edmiaston, R., & Sales, C. (2002). *Developing constructivist early childhood curriculum: Practical principles and activities.* New York: Teachers College Press.

Dickinson, D. K., & Tabors, P. O. (2002). Fostering language and literacy in classrooms and homes. *Young Children, 57*(2), 10–18.

Dodge, D. T., & Colker, L. (2002). *The Creative Curriculum for Early Childhood* (4th ed.). Washington, DC: Teaching Strategies, Inc.

Duckworth, E. (1987). *"The having of wonderful ideas" and other essays on teaching and learning.* New York: Teachers College Press.

Dunn, J., & Brown, J. (1991). Relationships, talk about feelings, and the development of affect regulation in early childhood. In J. Garber & K. A. Dodge (Eds.), *The development of emotion regulation and dysregulation* (pp. 89–108). New York: Cambridge University Press.

Dunn, J., Brown, J., & Beardsall, L. (1991). Family talk about feeling states, and children's later understanding of others' emotions. *Developmental Psychology, 27*(3), 448–455.

Dunsmore, J. C., & Halberstadt, A. G. (1997). How does family emotional expressiveness affect children's schemas? In K. C. Barrett (Ed.), *The communication of emotion: Current research from diverse perspectives* (New Directions for Child and Adolescent Development, no. 77, pp. 45–68). San Francisco: Jossey-Bass.

Early Childhood Equity Alliance. (2002). [Online: *www.RootsForChange.net*]

Edwards, C. P., Gandini, L., & Forman, G. E. (Eds.). (1998). *The hundred languages of children: The Reggio Emilia approach to early childhood education.* Norwood, NJ: Ablex.

Eisenberg, N. (1992). *The caring child.* Cambridge, MA: Harvard University Press.

Eisenberg, N. (2002). Emotion-related regulation and its relation to quality of social functioning. In W. Hartup & R. A. Weinberg (Eds.), *Child psychology in retrospect and prospect: In celebration of the seventy-fifth anniversary of the Institute of Child Development*, (Vol. 32, pp. 133–171). Mahwah, NJ: Erlbaum.

Eisenberg, N., & Fabes, R. A. (Eds.). (1992a). *Emotion and its regulation in early development*. San Francisco: Jossey-Bass.

Eisenberg, N., & Fabes, R. A. (1992b). Emotion regulation and the development of social competence. In M. S. Clark (Ed.), *Review of personality and social psychology: Vol. 14. Emotion and social behavior* (pp. 119–150). Newbury Park, CA: Sage.

Eisenberg, N., & Fabes, R. A. (1998). Prosocial development. In N. Eisenberg (Ed.), *Handbook of child psychology: Vol. 3. Social, emotional, and personality development* (5th ed., pp. 701–778). New York: Wiley.

Eisenberg, N., Losoya, S., Fabes, R. A., Guthrie, I. K., Reiser, M., Murphy, B., Shepard, S. A., Poulin, R., & Padgett, S. J. (2001). Parental socialization of children's dysregulated expression of emotion and externalizing problems. *Journal of Family Psychology, 15*(2), 183–205.

Eisenberg, N., & Valiente, C. (2002). Parenting and children's prosocial and moral dvelopment. In M. H. Bornstein (Ed.), *Handbook of parenting: Vol. 5. Practical issues in parenting* (2nd ed., pp. 111–142). Mahwah, NJ: Erlbaum.

Elicker, J., & Fortner-Wood, C. (1995). Research in review: Adult-child relationships in early childhood settings. *Young Children, 51*(1), 69–78.

Erikson, E. H. (1950). *Childhood and society*. New York: Norton.

Erikson, E. H. (1959). *Identity and the life cycle*. New York: Norton.

Evans, E. (1975). *Contemporary influences on early childhood education* (2nd ed.). New York: Holt, Rinehart & Winston.

Fabes, R. A., Eisenberg, N., Shepard, S., Guthrie, I., & Poulin, R. (1999). The role of regulation and emotionality in preschoolers' everyday socially competent peer interactions. *Child Development, 70*(2), 432–442.

Fabes, R. A., Hanish, L. D., Martin, C. L., & Eisenberg, N. (2002). Young children's negative emotionality and social isolation: A latent growth curve analysis. *Merrill-Palmer Quarterly, 48*(3), 284–307.

Fischer, K. W., Shaver, P. R., & Carnochan, P. (1990). How emotions develop and how they organise development. *Cognition and Emotion, 4*(2), 81–127.

Frede, E. C., Barnett, W. S., & Lupo, T. (2001). Measuring recommended practices for very young children with disabilities. In S. L. Golbeck (Ed.), *Psychological perspectives on early childhood education* (pp. 297–319). Mahwah, NJ: Erlbaum.

Galyer, K. T., & Evans, I. M. (2001). Pretend play and the development of emotion regulation in preschool children. *Early Child Development and Care, 166*, 93–108.

Garner, P. W., & Spears, F. M. (2000). Emotion regulation in low-income preschoolers. *Social Development, 9*(2), 246–264.

Gay, E., & Hyson, M. (1976). Blankets, bears, bunnies: Studies of children's contacts with treasured objects. In T. Shapiro (Ed.), *Psychoanalysis and contemporary science* (Vol. 5, pp. 271–316). New York: International Universities Press.

Georgia Office of School Readiness. (2001). *Georgia prekindergarten program: Learning goals*. Atlanta, GA: Author.

Gesell, A., Ilg, F. L., & Ames, L. B. (1995). Infant and child in the culture of today: The guidance of development in home and nursery school. Northvale, NJ: Jason Aronson. (Original published 1943)

Glenn Commission. (2000). *Before it's too late: A report to the nation from the National Commission on Mathematics and Science Teaching for the Twenty-first Century.* Washington, DC: U.S. Department of Education.

Goffin, S. G. (2001). Whither early childhood education in the next century? In L. Corno (Ed.), *Education across a century: The centennial volume* (pp. 140–163). National Society for the Study of Education (NSSE) Yearbook. Chicago: University of Chicago Press.

Gottman, J. M., Katz, L. F., & Hooven, C. (1996). *Meta-emotion: How famiies communicate emotionally, links to child peer relations, and other developmental outcomes.* Mahwah, NJ: Erlbaum.

Grace, C., & Shores, E. F. (1994). *The portfolio and its use: Developmentally appropriate assessment of young children* (3rd ed.). Little Rock, AR: Southern Association on Children Under Six.

Greenfield, P. M. (1994). Independence and interdependence as developmental scripts: Implications for theory, research, and practice. In P. M. Greenfield & R. R. Cocking (Eds.), *Cross-cultural roots of minority child development* (pp. 1–37). Hillsdale, NJ: Erlbaum.

Greenspan, S. I., & Greenspan, N. T. (1985). *First feelings: Milestones in the emotional development of your baby and child.* New York: Viking.

Greenspan, S. I., & Weider, S. (1998). *The child with special needs: Encouraging intellectual and emotional growth.* Reading, MA: Addison-Wesley.

Griffin, E. (1997). *Island of childhood: Education in the special world of nursery school.* New York: Educator's International Press.

Grossman, D. C., Neckerman, H. J., Koepsell, T. D., Liu, P. -Y., Asher, K. N., Beland, K., Frey, K., & Rivara, F. P. (1997). Effectiveness of a violence prevention curriculum among children in elementary school: A randomized controlled trial. *Journal of the American Medical Association, 277,* 1605–1611.

Guthrie, J. T., & Wigfield, A. (2000). Engagement and motivation in reading. In M. L. Kamil, P. B. Mosenthal, P. D. Pearson, & R. Barr (Eds.), *Handbook of reading research* (3rd ed.). New York: Longman.

Halberstadt, A. G. (1991). Toward an ecology of expressiveness: Family socialization in particular and a model in general. In R. S. Feldman & B. Rime (Eds.), *Fundamentals of nonverbal behavior* (pp. 106–160). New York: Cambridge University Press.

Halberstadt, A. G., Crisp, V. W., & Eaton, K. L. (1999). Family expressiveness: A retrospective and new directions for research. In P. Philippot & R. Feldman (Eds.), *The social context of nonverbal behavior: Studies in emotion and social interaction* (pp. 109–155). New York: Cambridge University Press.

Hale-Benson, J. E. (1986). *Black children: Their roots, culture, and learning styles.* Baltimore: Johns Hopkins University Press.

Hamre, B. K., & Pianta, R. C. (2001). Early teacher-child relationships and the trajectory of children's school outcomes through eighth grade. *Child Development, 72,* 625–638.

Hart, B., & Risley, T. (1999). *The social world of children learning to talk.* Baltimore: Paul H. Brookes.

Hartley, R. E., Frank, L. K., & Goldenson, R. M. (1952). *Understanding children's play.* New York: Columbia University Press.

Hartup, W. W., Laursen, B., Stewart, M. I., & Eastenson, A. (1988). Conflict and the friendship relations of young children. *Child Development, 59,* 1590–1600.

Head Start Bureau. (2001). Head Start child outcomes framework. *Head Start Bulletin,* no. 70. Washington, DC: Department of Health and Human Services, Administrator for Children and Families. Available on-line: *http://www. headstartinfo.org/publications/hsbulletin70/hsb70_15.htm*

Heath, S. B. (1983). *Ways with words: Language, life and work in communities and classrooms.* New York: Cambridge University Press.

Helm, J., & Beneke, S. (2003). *The power of projects: Meeting contemporary challenges in early childhood education classrooms.* New York: Teachers College Press & NAEYC.

Helm, J., Beneke, S., & Steinheimer, K. (1997). *Windows on learning: Documenting young children's work.* New York: Teachers College Press.

Helm, J., & Katz, L. (2001). *Young investigators: The project approach in the early years.* New York: Teachers College Press & NAEYC.

Henderson, H. A., & Fox, N. (1998). Inhibited and uninhibited children: Challenges in school settings. *School Psychology Review, 27*(4), 492–505.

Hendrick, J. (2000). *The whole child: Developmental education for the early years* (7th ed.). New York: Prentice-Hall.

High/Scope Staff (1992). *High/Scope Child Observation Record: For ages 2½–6.* Ypsilanti, MI: High/Scope Press.

Hirsh-Pasek, K., Hyson, M. C., & Rescorla, L. (1990). Academic environments in early childhood: Do they pressure or challenge young children? *Early Education and Development, 1*(6), 401–423.

Hoban, R. (1964). *Bread and jam for Frances.* New York: Harper & Row.

Hochschild, A. (1983). *The managed heart.* Berkeley: University of California Press.

Honig, A. S. (2002). *Secure relationships: Nurturing infant-toddler attachment in early care settings.* Washington, DC: NAEYC.

Howes, C. (1988). Peer interaction of young children. *Monographs of the Society for Research in Child Development, 53*(1, Serial No. 217).

Howes, C. (1992). *The collaborative construction of pretend: Social pretend play functions.* Albany: State University of New York Press.

Howes, C. (2000). Social-emotional classroom climate in child care, child-teacher relationships and children's second grade peer relations. *Social Development, 9*(2), 191–204.

Howes, C., & Ritchie, S. (2002). *A matter of trust: Connecting teachers and learners in the early childhood classroom.* New York: Teachers College Press.

Hymes, J. (1947). *A pound of prevention: How teachers can meet the emotional needs of young children.* New York: Teachers Service Committee on the Emotional Needs of Children.

Hyson, M. C. (1979). Lobster on the sidewalk: Understanding and helping children with fears. *Young Children, 34*(5), 49–60.

Hyson, M. C. (1996). Theory: An analysis (Part 2). In J. A. Chafel & S. Reifel (Eds.), *Advances in early education and day care: Theory and practice in early childhood teaching* (Vol. 8. pp. 41–89). Greenwich, CT: JAI Press.

Hyson, M. C. (2003). Putting early academics in their place. *Educational Leadership, 60*(7), 20–23.

Hyson, M. C., & Cone, J. (1989). Giving form to feeling: Emotions research and early childhood education. *Journal of Applied Developmental Psychology, 10*(3), 375–399.

Hyson, M. C., Hirsh-Pasek, K., & Rescorla, L. (1990). The Classroom Practices Inventory: An observation instrument based on NAEYC's "Guidelines for developmentally appropriate practices for 4- and 5-year-old children." *Early Childhood Research Quarterly, 5*(4), 475–494.

Hyson, M. C., & Lee, K. M. (1996). Assessing early childhood teachers' beliefs about emotions: Content, contexts, and implications for practice. *Early Education and Development, 7*(1), 59–78.

Hyson, M. C., & Molinaro, J. (2001). Learning through feeling: Children's development, teachers' beliefs and relationships, and classroom practices. In S. L. Golbeck (Ed.), *Psychological perspectives on early childhood education* (pp. 107–130). Mahwah, NJ: Erlbaum.

Hyson, M. C., Whitehead, L. C., & Prudhoe, C. (1988). Influences on attitudes toward physical affection between adults and children. *Early Childhood Research Quarterly, 3*(1), 55–75.

Isaacs, S. (1963). *Intellectual growth in young children.* New York: Schocken Books. (Original work published 1930)

Izard, C. E. (1991). *The psychology of emotions.* New York: Plenum.

Izard, C. E., Fine, S., Schultz, D., Mostow, A., Ackerman, B., & Youngstrom, E. (2001). Emotion knowledge as a predictor of social behavior and academic competence in children at risk. *Psychological Science, 12*(1), 18–23.

Izard, C. E., & Kobak, R. R. (1991). Emotions system functioning and emotion regulation. In J. Garber & K. A. Dodge (Eds.), *The development of emotion regulation and dysregulation* (pp. 303–321). New York: Cambridge University Press.

Johnson, H. M. (1928). *Children in the nursery school.* New York: John Day.

Jones, D. C., Abbey, B., & Cumberland, A. (1998). The development of display rule knowledge: Linkages with family expressiveness and social competence. *Child Development, 69,* 1209–1222.

Joseph, G. E., & Strain, P. S. (in press). Enhancing emotional vocabulary in young children. *Young Exceptional Children.*

Kamii, C. (2000). *Young children reinvent arithmetic: Implications of Piaget's theory* (2nd ed.). New York: Teachers College Press.

Kasari, C., & Sigman, M. (1996). Expression and understanding of emotion in atypical development: Autism and Down syndrome. In M. Lewis & M. W. Sullivan (Eds.), *Emotional development in atypical children* (pp. 109–130). Mahwah, NJ: Erlbaum.

Katz, L. (1995). *Talks with teachers of young children: A collection.* Norwood, NJ: Ablex.

Katz, L., & Chard, S. (2000). *Engaging children's minds: The project approach* (2nd ed.) Norwood, NJ: Ablex.

Katz, M. B. (1971). *Class, bureaucracy, and schools: The illusion of educational change in America.* New York: Praeger.

Kauffman Early Education Exchange. (2002). *Set for success: Building a strong foundation for school readiness based on the social-emotional development of young children.* Kansas City, MO: Ewing Marion Kauffman Foundation. Available on-line: *http://www.emkf.org*

Kelly, S. A., Brownell, C. A., & Campbell, S. B. (2000). Mastery motivation and self-evaluative affect in toddlers: Longitudinal relations with maternal behavior. *Child Development, 71*(4), 1061–1071.

Kilpatrick, J., Swafford, J., & Findell, B. (2001). *Adding it up: Helping children learn mathematics.* Washington, DC: National Academy Press.

Kitayama, S., & Markus, H. (Eds.). (1994). *Emotion and culture.* Washington, DC: American Psychological Association.

Klinnert, M. D., Campos, J. J., Sorce, J. F., Emde, R. N., & Svejda, M. (1983). Emotions as behavioral regulators: Social referencing in infancy. In R. Plutchik & H. Kellerman (Eds.), *Emotion: Theory, research, and experience: Vol. 2. Emotions in early development* (pp. 57–86). New York: Academic Press.

Kochanska, G., & Murray, K. T. (2000). Mother-child mutually responsive orientation and conscience development: Toddler to early school age. *Child Development, 71*(2), 417–431.

Kohlberg, L., & Mayer, R. (1972). Development as the aim of education. *Harvard Educational Review, 42*(4), 449–496.

Kopp, C. B. (1989). Regulation of distress and negative emotions: A developmental view. *Developmental Psychology, 25*(3), 343–354.

Kopp, C. B. (2002). School readiness and regulatory processes. In C. Raver (Ed.), Emotions matter: Making the case for the role of young children's emotional development for early school readiness. *Social Policy Report /* Society for Research in Child Development, *16*(3), 11.

Kusché, C. A. & Greenberg, M. T. (1994). *The PATHS Curriculum.* South Deerfield, MA: Channing L. Bete Co., Inc.

Kusché, C. A., & Greenberg, M. T. (in press). PATHS in your classroom: Promoting emotional literacy and alleviating emotional distress. In J. Cohen (Ed.), *Social emotional learning and the elementary school child: A guide for educators.* New York: Teachers College Press.

LaFreniere, P. J., & Dumas, J. E. (1995). *Social Competence and Behavior Evaluation: Preschool Edition (SCBE).* Los Angeles: Western Psychological Services.

Landy, S. (2002). *Pathways to competence: Encouraging healthy social and emotional development in young children.* Baltimore: Paul H. Brookes.

Lascarides, V. C., & Hinitz, B. F. (2000). *History of early childhood education.* New York: Falmer Press.

Leavitt, R. L. (1994). *Power and emotion in infant-toddler day care.* Albany: State University of New York Press.

Lemerise, E. A., & Arsenio, W. F. (2000). An integrated model of emotional processes and cognitiion in social information processing. *Child Development, 71*, 107–118.

Lewis, M. (1998). Emotional competence and development. In D. Pushkar & W. M. Bukowski (Eds.), *Improving competence across the lifespan: Building interventions based on theory and research* (pp. 27–36). New York: Plenum.

Lewis, M. (1999). The role of self in cognition and emotion. In T. Dalgleish & M. Power, (Eds.), *Handbook of cognition and emotion* (pp. 125–142). New York: Wiley.

Lewis, M., & Sullivan, M. E. (1996). *Emotional development in atypical children.* Hillsdale, NJ: Erlbaum.

Lutz, M. N., Fantuzzo, J., & McDermott, P. (2002). Multidimensional assessment of emotional and behavioral adjustment problems of low-income preschool children: Development and initial validation. *Early Childhood Research Quarterly, 17*(3) 338–335.

Lynch, E. W., & Hanson, M. J. (1998). *Developing cross-cultural competence: A guide for working with children and their families.* Baltimore: Paul H. Brookes.

Maguire, M. C., & Dunn, J. (1997). Friendships in early childhood, and social understanding. *International Journal of Behavioral Development, 21*(4), 669–686.

Mahler, M., Pine, F., & Bergman, A. (2000). *The psychological birth of the human infant.* New York: Basic Books.

Malatesta, C. Z., Culver, C., Tesman, J. R., & Shepard, B. (1989). The development of emotion expression during the first two years of life. *Monographs of the Society for Research in Child Development, 54*(1–2, Serial No. 219).

Malatesta, C. Z., & Haviland, J. M. (1982). Learning display rules: The socialization of emotion expression in infancy. *Child Development, 53*, 991–1003.

Malatesta-Magai, C. (1991). Development of emotion expression during infancy: General course and patterns of individual difference. In J. Garber & K. A. Dodge (Eds.), *The development of emotion regulation and dysregulation* (pp. 49–68). New York: Cambridge University Press.

Maryland State Department of Education. (2001). *Maryland's model for school readiness.* Annapolis, MD: Author.

McAdoo, H. P. (Ed.). (1997). *Black families* (3rd ed.). Newbury Park, CA: Sage Publications.

McAfee, O., & Leong, D. (2002). *Assessing and guiding young children's development and learning* (3rd ed.). Boston: Allyn & Bacon.

McMahon, R. J., & Conduct Problems Prevention Research Group. (in press). The prevention of conduct problems using targeted and universal interventions: The Fast Track Program. In D. Offord (Ed.), *Prevention of conduct disorder.* New York: Cambridge University Press.

Meisels, S., & Atkins-Burnett, S. (2002). The elements of early childhood assessment. In J. P. Shonkoff & S. J. Meisels (Eds.), *Handbook of early childhood intervention* (pp. 231–257). New York: Cambridge University Press.

Meisels, S., Liaw, F., Dorfman, A., & Nelson, R. F. (1995). The Work Sampling System: Reliability and validity of a performance assessment for young children. *Early Childhood Research Quarterly, 10*(3), 277–296.

Miller, A. M., & Harwood, R. L. (2001). Long-term socialization goals and the construction of infants' social networks among middle class Anglo and Puerto Rican mothers. *International Journal of Behavioral Development, 25*(5), 450–457.

Miller, P. H. (2002). *Theories of developmental psychology* (4th ed.) New York: Worth.

Missouri Department of Elementary and Secondary Education, Early Childhood Literacy Standards Committee. (2002). *Missouri preK literacy standards.* Jefferson City, MO: Author.

Moore, B. S. (1985). The behavioral consequences of affect. In M. Lewis & C. Saarni (Eds.), *The socialization of emotions* (pp. 213–237). New York: Plenum.

Moore, C., & Dunham, P. J. (Eds.). (1995). *Joint attention: Its origins and role in development.* Hillsdale, NJ: Erlbaum. Available on-line: *http://www.naeyc.org*

National Association for the Education of Young Children (NAEYC). (1995). *Position statement on responding to linguistic and cultural diversity.* Washington, DC: Author.

National Association for the Education of Young Children (NAEYC). (1996). *Pre-*

vention of child abuse in early childhood programs and the responsibilities of early childhood professionals to prevent child abuse [Position statement]. Washington, DC: Author. Available on-line: *http://www.naeyc.org*

National Association for the Education of Young Children (NAEYC). (1998). *Accreditation criteria and procedures of the National Association for the Education of Young Children,* 1998 edition. Washington, DC: Author.

National Association for the Education of Young Children (NAEYC). (2001). *Standards for Early Childhood Professional Preparation.* Washington, DC: Author.

National Association for the Education of Young Children (NAEYC) and National Association of Early Childhood Specialists in State Departments of Education (NAECS/SDE). (2002). *Early learning standards: Creating the conditions for success* [Position statement]. Washington, DC: NAEYC. Available on-line: *http://www.naeyc.org*

National Association for the Education of Young Children (NAEYC) and National Association of Early Childhood Specialists in State Departments of Education (NAECS/SDE). (2003). *Early childhood curriculum, child assessment, and program evaluation* [Position statement]. Washington, DC: NAEYC.

National Association for the Education of Young Children (NAEYC) and National Council of Teachers of Mathematics (NCTM). (2002). *Early childhood mathematics: Promoting good beginnings.* Washington, DC: NAEYC. Available on-line: *http://www.naeyc.org*

National Center for Education Statistics (NCES) (2002). *Children's reading and mathematics achievement in kindergarten and first grade.* Washington, DC: Author.

National Council of Teachers of Mathematics (NCTM). (2000). *Principles and standards for school mathematics.* Reston, VA: Author.

National Education Goals Panel. (1997). *Special early childhood report.* Washington, DC: Author.

Neuman, S., Copple, C., & Bredekamp, S. (2001). *Learning to read and write: Developmentally appropriate practices for young children.* Washington, DC: NAEYC.

Neuman, S. B., & Dickinson, D. K. (Eds.). (2001). *Handbook of early literacy research.* New York: Guilford Press.

Nyquist, E. B., & Hawes, G. R. (Eds.). (1972). *Open education.* New York: Bantam.

Olson, M., & Hyson, M. (2003). Supporting teachers, strengthening families: a new NAEYC initiative. *Young Children, 58*(3), 74–75.

Osborn, D. K. (1991). *Early childhood education in historical perspective* (3rd ed.). Athens, GA: Daye Press.

Owocki, G. (1999). *Literacy through play.* Portsmouth, NH: Heinemann.

Owocki, G. (2001). *Make way for literacy: Teaching the way young children learn.* Portsmouth, NH: Heinemann.

Parks, S. (1997). *Inside HELP: Administration and reference manual for the Hawaii Early Learning Profile.* Palo Alto, CA: VORT Corporation.

Peth-Pierce, R. (2000). *A good beginning: Sending America's children to school with the social and emotional competence they need to succeed.* Child Mental Health Foundations and Agencies Network (FAN) Monograph. Bethesda, MD: National Institute of Mental Health, Office of Communications and Public Liaison. Available on-line: *http://www.nimh.nih.gov/childhp/monograph.pdf*

Pianta, R. (Ed.). (1992). *Beyond the parent: The role of other adults in children's lives.* San Francisco: Jossey-Bass.

Pianta, R. (1999). *Enhancing relationships between children and teachers.* Washington, DC: American Psychological Association.

Pianta, R., La Paro, K., Payne, C., Cox, M. J., & Bradley, R. (2002). The relation of kindergarten classroom environment to teacher, family, and school characteristics and child outcomes. *Elementary School Journal, 102*(3), 225–238.

Polakow, V. (1992). *The erosion of childhood.* Chicago: University of Chicago Press.

Posada, G., Gao, Y., Wu, F., & Posada, R. (1995). The secure-base phenomenon across cultures: Children's behavior, mother's preferences, and experts' concepts. In E. Waters, B. E. Vaughn, G. Posada, & K. Kondo-Ikemura (Eds.), Caregiving, cultural, and cognitive perspectives on secure-base behavior and working models: New growing points of attachment theory and research. *Monographs of the Society for Research in Child Development, 60,* (2-3, Serial No. 244), 27–48.

Program for Infant/Toddler Caregivers. (2000). *Module I: Social-emotional growth and socialization.* San Francisco: WestEd.

Project Zero & Reggio Children. (2001). *Making learning visible: Children as individual and group learners.* Reggio Emilia, Italy: Reggio Children.

Ramsey, P. (1998). *Teaching and learning in a diverse world* (2nd ed.). New York: Teachers College Press.

Raspa, M. J., McWilliam, R. A., & Ridley, S. M. (2001). Child care quality and children's engagement. *Early Education and Development, 12*(2), 209–224.

Raver, C. (2002). Emotions matter: Making the case for the role of young children's emotional development for early school readiness. *Social Policy Report/*Society for Research in Child Development, *16*(3). Available on-line: *http://www.srcd.org/spr.html*

Raver, C., & Knitzer, J. (2002). *Ready to enter: What research tells policymakers about strategies to promote social and emotional school readiness among three- and four-year-old children.* New York: National Center for Children in Poverty, Columbia University Mailman School of Public Health. Available on-line: *http://cpmcnet.columbia.edu/dept/nccp/ProEmoPP3.html*

Redding, R. E., Morgan, G. A., & Harmon, R. J. (1988). Mastery motivation in infants and toddlers: Is it greatest when tasks are moderately challenging? *Infant Behaviour and Development, 11*(4), 419–430.

Renninger, K. A. (2000). Individual interest and its implications for understanding intrinsic motivation. In C. Sansone & J. M. Harackiewicz (Eds.), *Intrinsic and extrinsic motivation: The search for optimal motivation and performance* (pp. 373–404). San Diego, CA: Academic Press.

Renninger, K. A., Hidi, S., & Krapp, A. (Eds.). (1992). *The role of interest in learning and development.* Hillsdale, NJ: Erlbaum.

Repetti, R. L., Taylor, S. E., & Seeman, T. E. (2002). Risky families: Family environments and the mental and physical health of offspring. *Psychological Bulletin, 128*(2), 230–366.

Rogoff, B., & Morelli, G. (1989). Perspectives on children's development from cultural psychology. *American Psychologist, 44*(2), 334–348.

Rubin, K. H., Cheah, C. S. L., & Fox, N. (2001). Emotion regulation, parenting, and display of social reticence in preschoolers. *Early Education and Development, 12*(1), 97–115.

Russell, J. A. (1989). Costumes, scripts, and children's understanding. In C. Saarni

& P. L. Harris (Eds.), *Children's understanding of emotion* (pp. 293–318). New York: Cambridge University Press.

Saarni, C. (1990). Emotional competence: How emotions and relationships become integrated. In R. A. Thompson (Ed.), *Socioemotional development* (pp. 115–182). Lincoln: University of Nebraska Press.

Saarni, C. (1999). *The development of emotional competence.* New York: Guilford Press.

Saarni, C., Mumme, D. L., & Campos, J. (1998). Emotional development: Action, communication, and understanding. In W. Damon and N. Eisenberg (Ed.), *Handbook of child psychology: Social, emotional, and personality development* (5th ed., pp. 237–311). New York: Wiley.

Salovey, P., & Sluyter, D. J. (Eds.). (1997). *Emotional development and emotional intelligence: Educational implications.* New York: Basic Books.

Sandall, S., McLean, M., & Smith, B. (Eds.). (2000). *DEC recommended practices in early intervention/early childhood special education.* Longmont, CO: Sopris West.

Scholnick, E. K., Nelson, K., Gelman, S. A., & Miller, P. H. (Eds.). (1999). *Conceptual development: Piaget's legacy.* Mahwah, NJ: Erlbaum.

Schultz, D., Izard, C. E., Ackerman, B. P., & Youngstrom, E. (2001). Emotion knowledge in economically disadvantaged children: Self-regulatory antecedents and relations to social difficulties and withdrawal. *Development and Psychopathology, 13,* 53–67.

Schunk, D. H., & Zimmerman, B. J. (1997). Social origins of self-regulatory competence. *Educational Psychologist, 32*(4), 195–208.

Seefeldt, C., & Galper, A. (2002). *Active experiences for active children: Science.* Saddle River, NJ: Merrill/Prentice-Hall.

Sethi, A., Mischel, W., Aber, J. L., Shoda, Y., & Rodriguez, M. L. (2000). The role of strategic attention deployment in development of self-regulation: Predicting preschoolers' delay of gratification from mother-toddler interactions. *Developmental Psychology, 36*(6), 767–777.

Shapiro, M. S. (1983). *Child's garden: The kindergarten movement from Froebel to Dewey.* University Park: Pennsylvania State University Press.

Sharma, D., & Fischer, K. W. (Eds.). (1998). *Socioemotional development across cultures,* New Directions for Child Development, no. 81. San Francisco: Jossey-Bass.

Shaver, P., Schwartz, J., Kirson, D., & O'Conner, C. (2001). Emotion knowledge: Further exploration of a prototype approach. In W.G. Parrott (Ed.), *Emotions in social psychology: Essential readings* (pp. 26–56). Philadelphia, PA: Psychology Press/Taylor & Francis.

Shepard, L. A., Kagan, S. L., & Wurtz, E. (Eds.). (1998). *Principles and recommendations for early childhood assessments.* Washington, DC: National Education Goals Panel.

Shields, A., Dickstein, S., Siefer, R., Giusti, L., Magee, K., & Spritz, B. (2001). Emotional competence and early school adjustment: A study of preschoolers at risk. *Early Education and Development, 12*(1), 73–96.

Shields, A., & Cicchetti, D. (1998). Reactive aggression among maltreated children: The contributions of attention and emotion dysregulation. *Journal of Child Clinical Psychology, 27*(4), 381–395.

Shonkoff, J., & Meisels, S. (Eds.). (2000). *Handbook of early childhood intervention* (2nd ed.). New York: Cambridge University Press.

Shonkoff, J.P., & Phillips, D. (Eds.). (2001). From *neurons to neighborhoods: The science of early childhood development.* Washington, DC: National Academy Press.

Shure, M. (1992). *I can problem solve: An interpersonal cognitive problem-solving program*. Champaign, IL: Research Press.

Snow, C., Burns, S., & Griffin, P. (Eds.). (1999). *Preventing reading difficulties in young children*. Washington, DC: National Academy Press.

Spodek, B., & Saracho, O. (1996). Culture and the early childhood curriculum. *Early Childhood Development and Care, 12*(3), 1–14.

Squires, J., Bricker, D., & Twombly, E. (2001). *Ages and Stages Questionnaires: Social-Emotional (ASQ:SE)*. Baltimore: Paul H. Brookes.

Sroufe, L. A. (1996). *Emotional development: The organization of emotional life in the early years*. New York: Cambridge University Press.

State of Connecticut, State Board of Education. (1999). *Connecticut framework: Preschool curricular goals and benchmarks*. Hartford, CT: Author.

Steier, A. J., & Lehman, E. B. (2000). An observational measure of children's attachments to soft objects. *Child Study Journal, 30* (4), 253–271.

Stipek, D. J., & Greene, J. K. (2001). Achievement motivation in early childhood: Cause for concern or celebration? In S. L. Golbeck (Ed.), *Psychological perspectives on early childhood education* (pp. 64–91). Mahwah, NJ: Erlbaum.

Texas Education Agency. (1998). *Texas essential knowledge and skills for kindergarten*. Austin, TX: Author.

Thompson, R. A. (1994). Emotion regulation: A theme in search of a definition. *Monographs of the Society for Research in Child Development, 59*(2–3, Serial No. 240), 25–52.

Thompson, R. A. (2002). The roots of school readiness in social and emotional development. In Kauffman Early Education Exchange, *Set for success: Building a strong foundation for school readiness based on the social-emotional development of young children*. Kansas City, MO: Ewing Marion Kauffman Foundation.

Trevarthen, C., & Aitken, K. J. (2001). Infant intersubjectivity: Research, theory, and clinical applications. *Journal of Child Psychology and Psychiatry and Allied Disciplines, 42* (1), 3–48.

Walden, T. A., & Ogan, T. (1988). The development of social referencing. *Child Development, 59*, 1230–1240.

Walter, J. L., & LaFreniere, P. J. (2000). A naturalistic study of affective expression, social competence, and sociometric status in preschoolers. *Early Education and Development, 11*(1), 109–122.

Weber, E. (1969). *The kindergarten: Its encounter with educational thought in America*. New York: Teachers College Press.

Weber, E. (1984). Ideas influencing early childhood education: A theoretical analysis. New York: Teachers College Press.

Webster-Stratton, C., Reid, M. J., & Hammond, M. (2001). Preventing conduct problems, promoting social competence: A parent and teacher training partnership in Head Start. *Journal of Child Clinical Psychology, 30*(3), 283–302.

Worth, V. (1986). Tiger. In *Small poems again*. New York: Farrar, Straus, & Giroux. (Original work published 1975)

Zeanah, C. H., Boris, N. W., & Lieberman, A. F. (2000). Attachment disorders of infancy. In M. Lewis & A. J. Sameroff (Eds.), *Handbook of developmental psychopathology* (pp. 293–307). New York: Basic Books.

Zero to Three (1992). *Heart Start: The emotional foundations of school readiness*. Washington, DC: Author.

Index

About the Author

Marilou Hyson is Associate Executive Director for Professional Development at the National Association for the Education of Young Children (NAEYC). Before joining the staff of NAEYC in 2000, Hyson held a Society for Research in Child Development (SRCD) Executive Branch Policy Fellowship in the U.S. Department of Education's National Institute on Early Childhood Development and Education. Previously, she served as Professor and Chair of the Department of Individual and Family Studies at the University of Delaware and was Editor-in-Chief of *Early Childhood Research Quarterly*. Hyson received her Ph.D. in child development and early childhood education from Bryn Mawr College's Department of Education and Child Development. She has taught preschool and kindergarten children and directed a college-affiliated child care center. Her research projects, publications, and work at NAEYC have emphasized early emotional development, attitudes toward adult-child affection, the causes and effects of early academic expectations, and content and policy issues in early childhood teacher education, standards, and assessment.